THE BEST NEW U.S. & INTERNATIONAL

LABEL DESIGNS 2

Designed and Produced by:
Blount & Walker Visual Communications, Inc.
8771 Larwin Lane
Orlando, FL 32817
Telephone: (407) 677-6303
Fax: (407) 677-6487

Authors/Editors
Lisa Walker
Steve Blount

Publishers
Rockport Publishers
5 Smith St.
Rockport, MA 01966
(508) 546-9590

Distributed to the trade in the U.S. and Canada by:
North Light, an imprint of F&W Publications
1507 Dana Ave.
Cincinnati, OH 45207
(800) 289-0963
(513) 531-2222

Distributed to the trade throughout the rest of the world by:
Hearst Books International
105 Madison Ave.
New York, NY 10016
(212) 481-0355

Other distribution by:
Rockport Publishers
5 Smith St.
Rockport, MA 01966
Telex: 5106019284
Fax: (508) 546-7141

ISBN: 0-935603-31-X
Library of Congress Catalog Card Number: 87-60502

Printed in Japan by Dai Nippon Printing Co. Ltd.
Linotronic 300 output by Graphic Connexions, Cranbury, NJ

Design Credits/Chapter Openers:
Pg. 16: The Design Company
Pg. 17: Colonna, Farrell: Strategic Marketing & Design
Pg. 60: Pentagraph
Pg. 61: Elmwood Design Ltd.
Pg. 84: Michael Peters + Partners
Pg. 85: Pentagraph
Pg. 110: Colonna, Farrell: Strategic Marketing & Design
Pg. 111: Image Group, Inc.
Pg. 158: Mittleman/Robinson Design Associates
Pg. 159: Michael Peters + Partners
Pg. 176: Peterson & Blyth
177: Alan Chan Design Company
Pg. 204: Michael Peters + Partners
Pg. 205: Cato Design Inc.
Pg. 238: Kan Tai-keung Design & Associates Ltd.
Pg. 239: The Duffy Design Group

THE BEST NEW U.S. & INTERNATIONAL
LABEL DESIGNS 2

BY

Lisa Walker & Steve Blount

Rockport Publishers

Our sincere gratitude goes to the many design
firms and individual designers who lent their work
to the creation of this book. Time zone differences
and language barriers notwithstanding, they have
given generously of their time and talents to make
this new edition possible.

CONTENTS

INTRODUCTION

We hope this collection of new work will illuminate the many rapid changes taking place in visual communications and especially in product graphics.

In the three years since the release of our first book on packaging, *The Best New U.S. & International Label Designs*, product graphics have made a quantum leap, both in the quantity of new designs and —even more important—in their relative quality.

We received submissions literally from the ends of the Earth; all of the inhabited continents are represented. Our study of thousands of new designs was revealing. Especially in Europe and America, there seems to be a new boldness on the part of clients to encourage designers to go beyond the bounds of the safe and the accepted and reach for the exceptional. Clients also seem more willing to adopt identity programs that are subtler in concept and bolder in execution.

Designers tell us that clients have been influenced in this new openness by the attitudes of consumers. Television graphics and fashion in particular have become increasingly radical an eclectic. The product graphics this book reflect the growth of visual sophistication among buyers. That sophistication was evi-

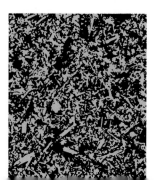

dent in the submissions chosen for the first edition as well, but it was largely confined to the so-called "upscale" market. Today, that same sophistication and the demand for intelligent, appropriate and pleasing graphics is evident at all levels of retail.

Increased sophistication and willingness to experiment may in part be natural consequences of consolidation and maturity in consumer markets. The number of new product categories being created has decreased; the number of new entries in existing categories has exploded. The result is a need for graphics which put greater emphasis on individuality in order to differentiate brands in crowded categories.

The visual trends we observed reflect a continuation of the internationalization of design, a strong resurgence of decoration as an acceptable esthetic, a multiple layering of images that has its roots in the Baroque tradition, and a confirmation that the design business is decentralizing.

There has been a strong surge in the billings, activity and the quality and diversity of output by shops located outside the tradi-tional design centers. New York, Paris and Tokyo are still home to the majority of the biggest design firms and the styles they popular-ize are still widely imitated. But the strong growth of regional de-sign centers and of firms outside of these established areas has greatly contributed to the growing diversity of product graphics. Their growth may, to some extent, be spurred by consumers' desire for variety and by the producers' need for differentiation.

Among these regional centers, San Francisco and Los Angeles exercise a stylistic influence that is felt all the way from Rome to the outer reaches of the Pacific Rim. The colors, shapes and styles favored by Californians have struck a responsive chord in con-sumers around the world.

California designers, due to the culture of the region and the atti-tudes of their clients, have some-times been able to experiment more freely. California artists were quick to adopt the Post-Modern esthetic and many of its stylistic tenets have become closely iden-tified with the state.

Consumers have come to as-sociate a freer, looser, more dec-orative graphic look with their own idealized view of California.

The Spanish explorers who made the west coast of North America known to Europeans took the name "California" from a mythical utopia created by a 16th-century Spanish novelist. In a time when expectations in much of the world are rising faster than the ability of the aver-age person to achieve them, utopias are an attractive com-modity. The lifestyle attributed to California—easy living, carefree and free spirited—might not be the reality experienced by the av-erage resident of Los Angeles or San Francisco. But, of course, it is not reality but the buyer's *per-ception* of reality that pries open pocketbooks. This misconception has been fostered and widely propagandized by the Hollywood entertainment establishment, help-ing California style become an important article of commerce around the world.

We hope this collection of new product graphics will help illumi-nate some of these changes tak-ing place in visual communica-tions and, especially, in the de-sign of product graphics. ♦

JACK ANDERSON

Far from being the low-priced stepsister of national brands, private label products have become superbrands in their own right, contributing mightily to retailers' image and bottom line.

*J*ack R. Anderson is a principal of Hornall Anderson Design Works, located in Seattle, Washington. Hornall Anderson produces a broad spectrum of print graphics, ranging from corporate identity to environmental signage and product packaging. The following was excerpted from an interview with Mr. Anderson. — Ed.

We've often been asked why the private-label program we created for Food Services of America is so elaborate. FSA provides foods for institutions—schools, hospitals, restaurants. Their products aren't primarily retail brands. So why do they, or any private label company, need such a complex identity?

The reason is simple: Consumers, whether they're stocking the home pantry or buying goods for a restaurant buffet, are looking for richness. They've become conditioned to designer foods, with rich images made up of multiple layers and four-color photographs of ingredients. They want their food to have a sophisticated look. In a package design, richness helps consumers get it—understand what they're buying. That's particularly true in food, and especially true for fruits and vegetables. When you walk into the more sophisticated supermarkets today, you see that the produce area has been really worked over. The overall lighting is less intense and they've positioned halide drop-lamps to shine right on the fruits and vegetables. The light put out by the lamps is very warm in color, and when they hit the vegetables and fruits, it produces a brilliant splash of color.

There's an emotional statement made about freshness and food. So if your product is in a can or a box, you're already fighting the preconception that it's canned; it's old, not fresh. It becomes even more important that the packaging say that the product is rich and high-quality.

There was a time when private label and institutional vendors created a corporate mark, a bug. And, usually, it was a nice mark. It looked good on a piece of stationery. But it didn't have any pizzazz or dressing. When it came time to put it on a can, they often just used the mark, and maybe a band of corporate color with some left-justified type. It ended up looking like auto parts or photographic products. When we audited the field, we found a number of vendors who were using what we call triple banding. All of their labels were of the same basic design. The company name appeared at the top and below it was a wide band of white where you could slug in the name of the product—"peas, thick syrup"— and at the bottom was a scruffy-looking four-color photo of what the product looked like.

They were paying for four-color reproduction, but weren't getting much out of it.

Conversely, some of the large private-label and institutional companies who also have retail brands—S&W, Del Monte —had moved to an enlarged version of their retail packaging. As consumers, most of us are brainwashed because we are looking at these products on our grocery shelves all the time. Those images have the same effect on us whether we're buying for ourselves or for a business.

So the bottom line for Food Services of America was that they needed a rich look that would go toe-to-toe with Del Monte's retail identity.

Food Services of America was a new company formed through the merger of two smaller firms. We began by creating a corporate identity and then moved into packaging as an extension of that. Our concept was to create a kit of "parts," of graphic pieces, which could be used in various combinations in a wide range of

applications,
from food packaging to stationery, business forms, delivery trucks, uniforms and signage.

The primary parts are the logo itself, a graduated tone—usually teal—and diagonal pinstripes. The logo (preceeding page) is a "shooting star." It actually started as a flag and evolved into a star. The flag stands for America, the star stands for quality, the wheat stalk in the center stands for food and the upward movement symbolizes growth. We gave it a somewhat technical feeling by virtue of the way it was rendered.

These elements were then transposed onto the packaging. Sometimes you see just the logo and the pinstripes, sometimes the pinstripes and a graduated tone, sometimes just a graduated tone. The look wasn't yuppie retail, but it had a little retail flair.

Anywhere we could print four-color offset, we did. We brought as many of the identity elements as we could onto the offset packages for number 10 cans, juice cans and large cartons. Where

we had to deal with products at lower prices, or where the graphics are printed directly on plastic bags, we couldn't get full process color. In those cases, the pinstripes became more important and we used a two-color illustration. The kit of parts had to be deep enough so that when we had to use the simplest form of reproduction —flexograph on cardboard —we could still use a graduated color and the lines and the logo to create a rich image.

Some of the elements we used for Food Services of America are purely decorative, but I think the days of creating one mark like the IBM logo and putting it in the upper right hand corner with twenty-five percent white space around it are over.

If you have a strong foundation, a logo or wordmark to serve as an anchor, you can pull these other pieces in and out to spice up the presentation and give it interest and variety. ♦

RALPH COLONNA

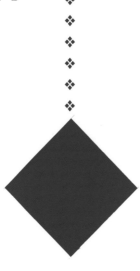

Graphics for consumer products have picked up a great deal of imagery from the wine business, and elegance and sophistication are definitely the order of the day.

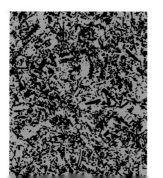

alph Colonna is a principal in the firm of Colonna, Farrell: Strategic Marketing and Design, St. Helena, California. The company is one of the most active firms in the field of wine label design throughout the U.S., Asia and Europe. In addition, Colonna, Farrell does a significant amount of work in other packaging categories and in corporate identity. In addition to the corporate design center in St. Helena, the firm has offices in New York and Los Angeles. The following is excerpted from an interview with Mr. Colonna. – Ed.

In the mid-1970s, packaging for the U.S. wine industry moved in a direction that played off of visual elements from other industries including cosmetics and European wine labels. This direction was noticeably different from that of packaging for other categories of products. The layering of visuals to form ever increasingly complex images and the use of fine-patterned backgrounds emerged. While these images were common in other fields of graphic design—such as annual reports—they weren't the *lingua Franca* for packaging. It wasn't the accepted norm since consumers did not readily understand the visual vocabulary of the style.

As wineries began to incorporate these new elements of design, consumers were quick to respond and understand that use of them implied "quality" and "attention to detail." Now we see these line patterns showing up in everything from paper towels to taco sauce. Today's market is divided—an extremely competitive market at the low end and another at the high end. As a producer, regardless of what your product is, you're looking for something that will boost your product up into the next category. A sophisticated label will help accomplish this.

Although it's difficult to make blanket predictions, for the next few years at least, the design vocabulary that will say sophistication to consumers will be simple and elegant. Jewelry and cosmetic graphics are good models—the simpler and more elegant the images are, the better. You'll probably still see the Baroque style of layering images, but each image will work more ef-fectively with the other and overall images are going to be simpler.

Another design element that will grow in popularity over the next two to five years with wines is the use of more individualized glass shapes. This has been made possible by the advent of short-run glass containers from Europe. If you're willing to pay for the tooling costs up front, you can order as few as 3,000 cases of wine bottles made to unique and interesting specifications. Of course, we are seeing these bottles appear in the sparkling wine market because producers of this type of wine usually have larger budgets for packaging. Even still wines are being packaged in uniquely-shapes bottles and bottles decorated with a crest.

California vintners appear to be more willing to break away from the traditional European shapes, but they may still be somewhat skeptical of getting too far off the traditional path. Cost is a primary factor. Mass market producers can't afford custom glass; short run producers are likely to be more inventive. Reflecting greater self-confidence, California wineries now set their own standards. Traditional Chardonnays—big, fat and buttery—are fast being replaced by a light and airy Chardonnay style. This is another example of California saying, "We can set our own standards and patterns."

The influence from California

PAPER
SELECTION

Just as every wine has its own personality, the design of a wine label requires the designer to satisfy a number of different personalities. Each of the many persons involved in bringing a wine to market has his own prejudices and his own point to make about the product. Designers at Colonna, Farrell created these bottles to provide an amusing and whimsical illustration of the conflicting desires of the various participants and design elements that complicate the process.

VINTAGE 1980 BOTTLED

BOTTLE
SHAPE

COLOR

ARTIST
WINE

CHEAPO
Primo

CONTAINS SULFITES

DIE-CUT

seems to extend across the Pacific. Most of the Pacific Rim—not just Asia, but New Zealand, Australia and South America as well—looks to California as a wonderful kind of Utopia. Although it may not be, they respond well to what they think the California image is. This is not necessarily the case with other parts of the U.S. that produce varietal wines, especially the Long Island region of New York. Labels for these wines are designed primarily in New York City, and there's a certain look to them that's different from California. The Pacific Northwest might be described as having a more homespun style; not quite as sophisticated as labels done in California or New York. We're trying to encourage that sort of regional identity for wines. There's no reason for a Long Island wine to look like one produced in California.

Like the wines themselves, the growing regions are creating their own graphic personalities. This is appropriate because we design wine labels to fit a person or company's image rather than some arbitrary image we might conjure up. After all, that's what sells the wine. If we put too much of our image into it, we won't be saying enough about the wine. What may be effective for one wine or class of wine may not work for another.

Mass market wineries such as Round Hill and Glen Ellen have their niche in grocery stores and mass retail outlets. These labels are produced much like any other consumer product. It has to hit hard and have good shelf appeal since the wines are usually displayed en masse. We try to design them so that when you get six or ten facings of the brand, a nice pattern emerges. For a mass market wine, we try to quickly communicate the name of the varietal and some visual identifiers that will say this is the best product for the price.

At the other end of the scale, there are wines such as Beringer Private Reserve or Heublein's Gustave Niebaum Collection. These labels are much more subtle and designed to be sold primarily in exclusive wine shops and better restaurants where a strong shelf presence isn't needed. In this case, the buyers are knowledgeable about wines. They buy because of the year or the style of a particular wine maker. The label can be designed in layers resulting in a first, second and third reading. As you look at the label, several things happen. Type that is very small or light in color doesn't read until you pick up the bottle. Background patterns that look like water markings in the paper from a distance may be the logo of the winery; what looks like a single border from two feet away becomes multiple, intricate borders as you get closer.

Often these wines have to be designed not only for retail, but to look grand on a restaurant table as well. We have to design for a variety of lighting schemes and environmental scales.

Everyone has their own idea of how to handle the market. This is probably the only category I know of where you can work for competing companies. The differences in this market flow from the many personalities—the winery, the wine maker, the region and the grapes themselves—and that's the fun of designing wine labels.

An interesting—and revealing—change that has taken place in the packaging of foods is the virtual disappearance of gourmet foods as a separate and distinct visual category.

Differences between products to be sold in supermarkets and those destined for the shelves of gourmet shops were once obvious and predictable. The traditional messages used to sell gourmet foods—high quality, handmade, expensive—are now being used to market all types of foods. Paper overwraps, ribbons, die-cut hang tags, faux wax seals, foil stamping and other expensive post-production touches have been added to everything from orange juice to frozen entrees (which, not too long ago, were called TV dinners).

Some of the pressures forcing food packaging to be "upscale" include crowding of established food categories with new brands, rather than new products; the diminishing difference in cost between the lowest- and highest-priced items in many categories and the resulting need to create a distinction based on perceived quality; and increasing visual sophistication on the part of the consumer. Even for items where the buying decision is made on the basis of price, consumers seem to be demanding what was once called a boutique look. As one designer put it, "people now care about *all* of their purchases." ♦

FOODS

Gourmet used to be a special —and identifiable—style. But complex, multi-layered graphics have become the norm on food products ranging from frozen burritos to beer nuts.

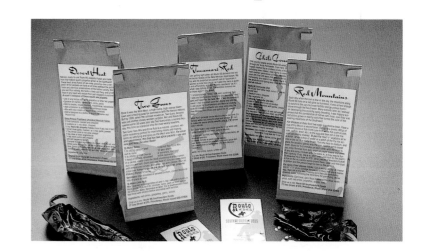

▲ **Route 66 Southwestern Foods.**
Design Firm: **The Design Company**

Route 66 spices and mixes
bring an authentic Southwestern taste to ethnic dishes. Marketed to small convenience and
specialty foods stores, the package needed to capture the look
of the old Southwest yet appeal
to a contemporary audience.
Printed in two PMS colors and
one Toyo ink on white litho label
stock. The pencil drawing was
printed as a halftone to give the
background an old-fashioned
look.

❖ **Ti'Light** for **Raffineries Tirlemontoises.** Design Firm: **Design Board Behaeghel & Partners;** Art Director: **Denis Keller;**
Designer/Illustrator: **Sally Swart**

Ti'Light is a "light" sugar product, each serving containing
about one-third less calories
than a lump of sugar. The
brush-stroke illustration projects
a contemporary image, while
the stark white background
suggests that this is a "light"
product.

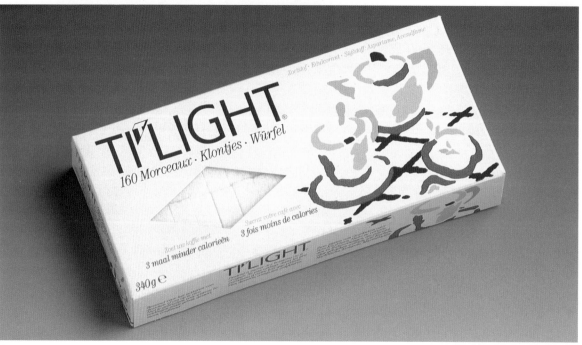

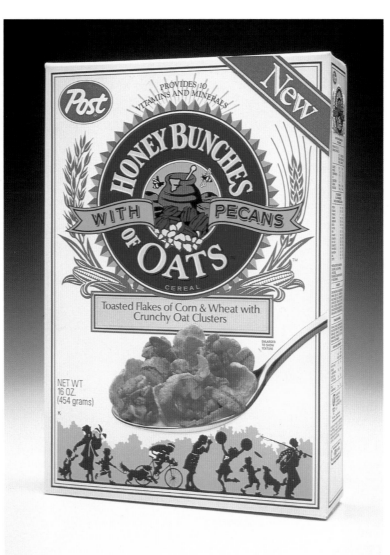

Honey Bunches of Oats Cereal for **Post/General Foods.** Design Firm: **SBG Partners;** Art Director/Designer: **Barry Deutsch;** Illustrators: **Hank Osuna, Liz Kenyon**

Honey Bunches of Oats is a new cereal positioned as a "fun" breakfast food for the entire family. The focal point of the package—the circular brand mark flanked on either side by stalks of grain—takes care of the usual selling points: it's natural, it's good for you, it tastes good. Silhouetted images along the bottom hint at the "fun" aspects of the product.

Lindberg-Snider BBQ Sauces for **Lindberg-Snider.** Design Firm: **Harte Yamashita & Forest;** Art Director/Designer: **Susan Healy**

Lindberg Snider markets their BBQ Sauces & Marinades to independent butchers, food stores and specialty shops. The graphics project the natural and homestyle qualities of the products, while maintaining a value-priced position. Printed in four colors by flexography on self-adhesive label stock.

▲ Christmas gift for **Libby Perszyk Kathman.** Design Firm: **Libby Perszyk Kathman;** Art Director/Designer: **John Metz**

Libby Perszyk Kathman of Cincinnati, Ohio, uses holiday gifts as a way to demonstrate its versatility in package design. The label graphics featured at right reflect the attention to detail and quality graphics available at the studio.

❖ Christmas gift for **Libby Perszyk Kathman.** Design Firm: **Libby Perszyk Kathman;** Art Director/Designer: **Susan Bailey Zinader;** Illustrator: **Jane McIlvain**

Another variation on the holiday theme. This hand-packed honey is the fourth in a series of holiday gifts promoting Libby Perszyk Kathman's design capabilities.

▲

❖

Scottish Salmon for Joseph Johnston & Sons. Design Firm: Graphic Partners; Art Director: Ron Burnett; Designer: Sean Gibbs

Joseph Johnston is an established supplier of high-quality smoked salmon to the wholesale market. Graphic Partners was commissioned to produce a new logo and identity program for private label products that would retain the equity of the existing trademark. Printed on a letterpress in three colors on self-adhesive stock with a varnish.

▲ Oils for **Consilia**. Design Firm: **Michael Peters + Partners**; Art Director: **Pat Perchal**; Designer: **Barry Gillibrand**; Illustrator: **Harry Willock**

Brilliant botanical illustrations printed by litho onto tin plate add appetite appeal to this line of Consilia vegetable oils. The use of cans, rather than the clear bottles more common in the U.S., adds to the product's shelf life and gives the designers an unusual background for the graphics.

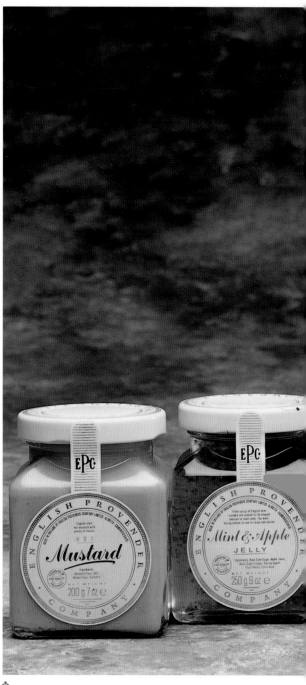

❖ Labels for **English Provender Company**. Design Firm: **Elmwood Design Ltd.**; Designer: **Julia White**

In packaging the English Provender line of condiments, flower waters and vinegars for the gift market, Elmwood Design chose an elegant typographic approach rather than relying on the rustic, countrified graphics often seen on these items.

■ **Presidio Gourmet Sauces** for **Sauces Unlimited**. Design Firm: **Taylor/Christian Advertising**; Designers: **Roger Christian, Elaine Lytle**

Gift-packed gourmet sauces are ubiquitous. This line of Mexican-style picanté sauces uses a stylized cactus to capture a bit of the Southwest. The labels are printed offset in four colors on 70-pound Champion Carnival Groove Offset stock.

Tomatoes, Water, Onions, Jalapeno Peppers, Bell Peppers, Vinegar, Salt, Carrots, Garlic, Cilantro.

GOURMET PICANTE SAUCE

P R E S I D I O

On any given day, Presidio, a town of 800 near the Mexican border in west Texas, is the hottest place on earth. This classic example of Tex-Mex culture is the namesake for the greatest Picante Salsa ever made. A blend of ripe tomatoes, mild jalapeno peppers, onions, bell peppers, carrots and cilantro. Simply put, Presidio is the best we can make. Put it on everything.

Sauces Unlimited, Inc.
P.O. Box 37385
San Antonio, TX 78237

™   Net Weight 12.0 oz.

▲ **Ahh Shucks Microwave Popcorn on the Cob** for **Story's Gourmet Foods, Inc.** Design Firm: **Lane/Mazzone & Associates;** Designers: **Ray Lane, Rae Ann Cirrito, Jaime McPherson**

This colorful label wraps around a glass Fido jar filled with eight earns of corn, shucks and all. Contrasting teal color ink provides a slightly contemporary diversion to the warm earth tones. Die-cut and printed in six colors with a varnish on 60-pound Fasson Satin Litho Removable stock.

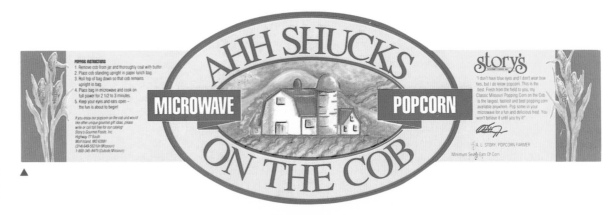

❖ **Maurice et Charles Vinaigrette** for **Maurice Amzallag.** Design Firm: **Colonna, Farrell: Strategic Marketing & Design;** Art Director: **Ralph Colonna;** Designer: **Susan Handly;** Copywriter: **Richard Clark**

These natural vinaigrette dressings have been served at the Maurice et Charles Restaurant, located in San Rafael, California, for more than 15 years. The line includes more than eight varieties, all featuring a stylized label decked out in France's national colors. The bright red neck band provides a pleasing visual contrast to the neutral color liquid.

Strombito for **Telesco's.** Design Firm: **Tharp Did It;** Art Director: **Rick Tharp;** Designers: **Kim Tomlinson, Rick Tharp;** Illustrator: **Kim Tomlinson**

The labels are well designed in many respects, but we especially like the whimsical illustrations that identify each variety—a mushroom for the vegetable strombito, a pizza maker for the meat and cheese variety. Designers Kim Tomlinson and Rick Tharp had to fit in what seems to be a lot of product copy, but kept the presentation from looking dense by printing type in different colors and placing a drop shadow behind the product name to give it some dimension. Note that the drop shadow is made up of horizontal lines—not a dot screen—to maximize available white space.

▲ Grain gift packs for **Fantastic Foods**. Design Firm: **Rene Yung Communications Design Inc.**; Art Director/Designer: **Rene Yung**

Five years ago, grains and pasta would hardly have been thought of as gift items in America. Giving a box of basmati for a birthday just wasn't done. Now it seems perfectly natural for finest-quality items—no matter what food group they belong to—to be dressed up in gift boxes and ribbons.

❖ **Highland Fayre**. Design Firm: **Graphic Partners**; Art Director/Designer: **Ron Burnett;** Illustrator: **Ann Ross Paterson**

Highland Fayre is a small mailorder firm which makes Scottish specialty foods. Though the budget was not lavish, Graphic Partners managed to create an identity that is obviously, but discretely, Scottish. Labels for the range of marmalades are identical, with product varieties overprinted in black to minimize production costs. The design garnered a Clio in the international division for 1989.

■ **San Antonio River Mills** labels for **Pioneer Flour Mills**. Design Firm: **WRK, Inc.;** Art Director/Designer/Illustrator: **Michelle Knauss**

Another solution for mail order foods, WRK's designs for San Antonio River Mills make use of a variety of outer packages. All share a strong logo and common color scheme. The labels are printed in four colors on pressure-sensitive stock.

▲ **Black Angus Beef** sticker for **Misty Isle Farms**. Design Firm: **Hornall Anderson Design Works;** Art Director: **Jack Anderson;** Designers: **Jack Anderson, Julie Tanagi;** Illustrator: **Mary Hermes**

Meat is meat—unless it's Misty Isle, custom-cut grain-fed beef. To get this point across to consumers, Misty Isle Farms commissioned Hornall Anderson to create a sticker that could be affixed to fresh cuts of meat wrapped in butcher's paper. Black Angus cattle produce the highest-quality beef; an illustration of a Black Angus steer underscores the source of the meat.

❖ **Select Servings** for **Foster Farms**. Design Firm: **Primo Angeli Inc.;** Creative Director: **Primo Angeli;** Designers: **Rolando Rosler, Doug Hardenburgh**

This colorful packaging would be a standout in any poultry cooler—most of which are a vast expanse of see-through shrink wrap and peach-colored meat. The largest producer of fresh chicken in the western U.S., Foster Farms created a new category of fresh chicken product it calls Select Servings. The chicken is marinated in one of several sauces and packed in a microwave-safe container. The packaging had to suggest that the dishes were quick, yet natural and of gourmet quality. A small die-cut window just above the variety name lets consumers see the fresh meat inside.

SPRING MOUNTAIN
N·A·P·A · V·A·L·L·E·Y

WALNUTS

SPRING MOUNTAIN WALNUT COMPANY
4003 SPRING MTN. ROAD, ST. HELENA, CA 94574, (707) 963-4233
NET WT. 1 LB.

■ Labels for **Spring Mountain Walnuts**. Design Firm: **Colonna,Farrell: Strategic Marketing & Design;** Art Director: **Ralph Colonna;** Designer: **Amy Racina;** Illustrator: **Mike Gray**

High in the Sierra Nevada, luxurious walnuts are packed by Spring Mountain. The nuts are sold in gourmet stores, and the firm needed a label that would work on both large burlap bags and small cellophane bags.

● Sauces for **Eden Foods, Inc**. Design Firm: **Perich & Partners;** Art Director/Designer: **Janine Thielk;** Calligrapher: **Ikuko Takahashi.**

Soy sauce is never just soy sauce, as the Eden Foods line shows. The five varieties are designated by color coding, with "Traditional Japanese" added to distinguish the imported sauces from the domestic American ones. The hand-drawn characters point up the Oriental origin of the sauces. The labels are printed in five colors on metallic stock.

▲ **Creme Supreme** specialty cheese for **Love At First Bite.** Design Firm: **Rene Yung Communications Design Inc.;** Art Director/Designer: **Rene Yung;** Typography: **Display Lettering & Copy**

Making the transition from specialty food store to supermarket is easier for some products than for others. Cheese is one food product that easily makes the transition. This elegant packaging system and brand identity program clearly positions the product as a premium quality, delicately rich cheese.

❖ Rice for **California Korea Rice Company.** Design Firm: **Image Group, Inc.;** Art Director/Designer/Illustrator: **Karen Lim;** Film Work & Printing: **Bemis Bag Company**

Three rice products, three distinctive Oriental looks that appeal to the target audience—Koreans living in the U.S. Baek Jo Calrose Rice (left) features a white swan to let consumers know that the product is pure. Jang Soo Brown Rice (center) combines the traditional Korean salutation of "good health" with the ancient Chinese character denoting longevity. Chung Ja New Variety Rice (right), capitalizes on the royal heritage of the Chung Ja name to project an upscale image. All bags are printed in four colors.

WE KNOW YOU REMEMBER THE
STORY. THE CHANT AND
CHASE ARE ETCHED INDELIBLY INTO
OUR COLLECTIVE MEMORY. WE
ALSO KNOW THAT GINGERBREAD MEN
INSPIRE CHILDHOOD RITUALS
THAT LAST A LIFETIME.
DO YOU BITE OFF THE HEAD FIRST,
OR THE LITTLE FEET? DO YOU
PULL OUT RAISIN EYES, POP OFF
CANDY BUTTONS, OR
DEVOUR YOUR COOKIE IN ONE
GIANT BITE?

DON'T BE ASHAMED. THESE
LITTLE FELLOWS BRING OUT THE FOX
IN EVERYONE. PERHAPS
THERE'S SOMETHING JUST A LITTLE
TOO GOOD IN THAT SILKY,
AROMATIC DOUGH. PERHAPS WE CAN'T
HELP BUT REMEMBER THAT
LEGENDARY CHALLENGE:
"RUN, RUN, AS FAST AS YOU CAN…"

PHILLIPS DESIGN GROUP
WOULD LIKE TO PRESENT YOU WITH A
CHALLENGE. DON'T BE FOOLED—
IT SEEMS DECEPTIVELY SIMPLE.
BAKE A BATCH OF GINGERBREAD MEN
FOR YOUR FAMILY AND FRIENDS.
DECORATE THEM AS YOU LIKE.
LET YOUR IMAGINATION RUN WILD
AND CREATE THE GINGERBREAD MEN
OF YOUR DREAMS–OR NIGHTMARES.
THEN, SEND US ONE COOKIE.
WE PROMISE WE WON'T LET HIM GET
AWAY–AND HE MAY TURN UP
AGAIN. SO, WE HOPE YOU'LL ROLL UP
YOUR SLEEVES AND ACCEPT OUR
CHALLENGE. THIS IS YOUR CHANCE
TO SHOW US WHAT YOU'RE MADE OF,
AND ONE DESIGN PROJECT WE'RE
LEAVING TO OUR FRIENDS.

■ Self-promotional Gingerbread Cookie Tin. Design Firm: **Phillips Design Group;** Art Director: **Scott J. Ward;** Designers: **Alison Moritsugu, Julie Haynes, Mary Head;** Illustrator: **Alison Moritsugu**

Each holiday season Phillips Design Group makes a Christmas gift for friends and clients. This gingerbread tin contained cookie cutters, mix and sprinkles—all the ingredients needed to bake creative cookies. A recipe helps newcomers along. Labels are printed in four Toyo inks with spot varnish on Fasson Crack-n-Peel stock (#55 Gloss Enamel, Brite-White Semi-Gloss).

▲ **A La Francais Yogurt** for **H.J. Heinz Co.** Design Firm: **Libby Perszyk Kathman;** Art Director/ Designer/Illustrator: **Jim Gabel**

Packaging for Weight Watcher's low-calorie foods has come a long way since the familiar pink boxes. New color schemes and contemporary graphics reach out beyond the core audience—women. This effort by Libby Perszyk Kathman meets the goals of the assignment: that the package communicate appetite appeal and a contemporary image. Notice that the Weight Watchers name is still featured, but it wasn't given center stage.

❖ **Cracker Barrel Cheese** for **Kraft Limited.** Design Firm: **Andrew Bell Graphic Designers Pty. Ltd.;** Designer: **Andrew Bell**

Who doesn't remember sitting in the kitchen stacking Cracker Barrel Cheese slices on crackers, topping them with heaps of spicy mustard? Andrew Bell incorporated some of the recognizable icons of the old packaging into these new wrappers. Block-style lettering hints of the product's heritage, while angled lines give it a whole new look.

▲

❖

Goats' Milk Yoghurt and **Goats' Milk Cream** for **Scottish Goat Products Ltd.** Design Firm: **Graphic Partners;** Art Director: **Ken Craig;** Designer: **Jenny Smith;** Illustrator: **Ann Ross Paterson**

In 1986 the Scottish Goat Products Marketing Cooperative was established to promote the various goats' milk products produced by small herds of goats throughout Scotland. Though the products are of high quality and an excellent alternative to cow's milk, many consumers believe goats' milk is unsanitary. The graphics had to project a clean, hygienic image. Freshness, quality and purity are emphasized through a careful choice of primary colors and a free, fluid calligraphic illustration rendered against a brilliant white background. The Goatherd packaging was a finalist in the international competition of the 1989 Clio awards.

▲ **Mango Lime Caribbean Conserve** for **Oualie Foods.** Design Firm: **Clifford Selbert Design;** Art Director/Designer/Illustrator: **Susan Turner**

In the United States, Caribbean cuisine hasn't reached the status of Mexican or Italian fare, but Caribbean style is everywhere—in graphics, textiles, interior design. One of six Caribbean-inspired specialty and snack items, these conserves are dressed in a delightful label sporting the graphics and hot colors of the islands. The new line debuted in September 1989, with projected sales of $800,000 in the first year. Labels are printed in four colors.

❖ **Nori** packaging for **Yamaiso Co.** Art Director/Designer: **Shigeru Akizuki**

A stark contrast to the graphics of the Caribbean, the package design for this Nori product—a traditional dish of Japan—is just as striking. An illustration of a wave depicts that this is a product of the sea.

■ **Mary's Pizza Salad Dressing** for **Mary's Pizza Shack.** Design Firm: **Colonna, Farrell: Strategic Marketing & Design;** Art Director: **Ralph Colonna;** Designer: **Amy Racina;** Illustrator: **Beth Whybrow Leeds;** Copywriter: **Richard Clark;** Printer: **Calistoga Press**

That's a picture of Mary, the owner of the well-known restaurant, Mary's Pizza Shack, and producer of this wholesome sauce. Located in the Sonoma Valley of California, the family-owned restaurant sells this concoction for use as a sauce, dressing or marinade.

Label graphics for products that sell in both gourmet stores and supermarkets have to be appropriate to both environments. Not all are. Some labels are too refined for a supermarket shelf; others are too commercial looking. These labels could easily make the transition from gourmet store to supermarket. The diamond-shape symbol above the name plays on the client's name. The earthy color scheme and simplistic illustrations would fare well in a variety of retail formats.

▲ **ANF Dog Foods** for **Martha White Foods Inc.** Design Firm: **Primo Angeli Inc.;** Creative Director: **Primo Angeli;** Designers: **Vicki Cero, Ray Honda**

ANF makes a range of top-quality dog food sold to "serious pet owners" through pet food shops and specialty feed outlets. The client wanted a package/label design that positioned the chow as "The Best of the Best"—a concept underscored in the circular graphic above the label. No-nonsense graphics appeal to pet owners who are serious about feeding their pets quality nutritional food.

❖ **Perform** pet foods for **Carnation Company.** Design Firm: **Harte Yamashita & Forest;** Art Director/Designer: **Denise Georgeson;** Illustrator: **Karen Bell**

Perform was the first national brand of dog and cat food (both wet and dry) sold through direct mail. The graphics were intended to position the brand as premium, all natural pet food. The bags are printed in five colors by rotogravure with a gloss varnish. Offset lithography labels are printed five colors with a matte varnish.

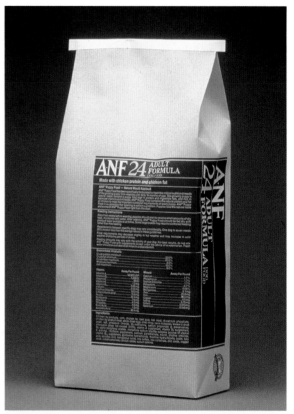

▲

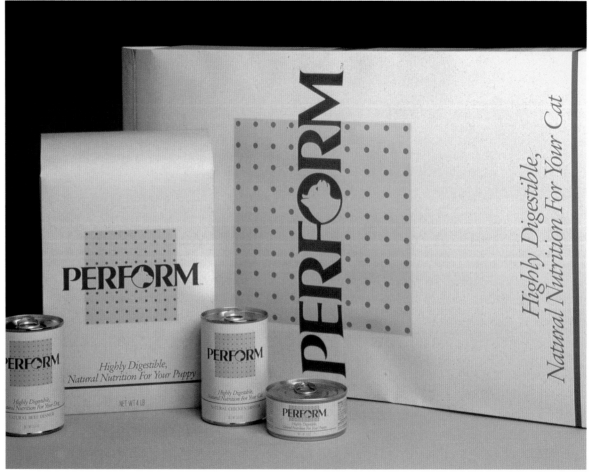

❖

■ **Mox Lox Sea Legs** for **Berelson Company.** Design Firm: **Bright & Associates;** Art Director: **Keith Bright;** Designer: **Wilson Ong**

The Berelson Company was one of the first to import Surimi (imitation seafood) into the U.S. Because the products are distributed to both the retail and foodservice industries, the packaging was designed to work in both arenas. Each product line is color-coded for easy identification in storage cabinets and on the shelf. Bright & Associates incorporated the "bagel and lox" illustration on the Mox Lox package to increase appetite appeal and promote the well-known serving suggestion.

● Vegetables for **Consilia.** Design Firm: **Michael Peters + Partners;** Art Director: **Pat Perchal;** Designers: **Pat Perchal, Fiona Warn;** Illustrator: **Harry Willock**

Consilia Vegetables is a private label brand. Instead of color-coding the label, the designers let the actual colors of the products identify the varieties. A tab hangs over the lid to underscore the impression of quality.

▲ **Cajun King Sauce Mixes** for **Bruce Foods Corp.** Design Firm: **Axion Design Inc.;** Art Director: **James McElheron;** Designer: **Lisa Brussell;** Illustrators: **Linda Bacon, Nancy Wagstaff;** Photographer: **William Turner**

A lot of visual focal points are worked into the front of this package: A stylized logo, four-color photo, dog ear copy and product type. The design team was able to keep the design from looking cluttered by varying typeface styles and weights. A nice, clean presentation.

❖ **Classico Pasta Sauce** for **Prince Foods.** Design Firm: **The Duffy Design Group;** Art Director: **Charles S. Anderson;** Designers/Illustrators: **C. Anderson, H. Johnson**

In keeping with the memorable style of the original Classico labels, these labels for new varieties of the pasta sauce feature a "nuovo" stamp and a new color palette. Printed in four colors and one match color on speckletone natural text stock.

■ **Jintan Breath Mints** for **Morishita Jintan Co.** Art Director/Designer: **Shigeru Akizuki**

Tokyo designer Shigeru Akizuki always tries to incorporate some kind of imagery into his work. For these breath mints, the circular shape symbolizes a mouth, and the graduated color tones depict breath.

● **Food packaging** for **Williams-Sonoma.** Design Firm: **SBG Partners;** Art Director/Designer: **Courtney Reeser**

SBG Partners created a sleek black package design system to unify the various private label foods sold by this specialty retailer. A circular corporate mark ghosted behind the product name and bright red symbols of the various foods make each package look unique.

▲ **Dip, Dressing and "Nayonaise" for Nasoya Foods.** Design Firm: **Selame Design;** Art Director: **Joe Selame;** Designers: **Selame Design Group**

This an excellent example of an eye-catching graphic system that can be adapted to a variety of package sizes and shapes. Nasoya Foods manufactures soy-based foods that contain no cholesterol. With a growing line of products, the company wanted a unifying look. The checkerboard motif and casual style of illustration are striking in their simplicity. Containers for the dips are printed in three or four special match colors on white plastic tubs. Labels for the dressings are printed in four special match colors on white coated stock. Labels for Nayonaise are printed in five special match colors on white coated stock.

❖ **Firehouse Bar-B-Que Sauce** for **Firehouse Bar-B-Que.** Design Firm: **John Haag Design;** Art Director/Designer: **John Haag**

Originally, labels for Firehouse Bar-B-Que Sauce featured an illustration of the company's founder. But his recent departure from the firm presented an opportunity to redesign the label. The headshot was replaced with an illustration of a fire hat, and the word "sauce" was incorporated into the oval-shaped motif. The background color was changed to bold red for added shelf impact. The results? Sales are up dramatically, according to designer John Haag. Three colors differentiate each flavor: Black for Rich & Zesty; yellow for Hot & Spicy; and orange for Real Hot.

■ **Beef for Fajitas** for **Texas Western Beef.** Design Firm: **Ruenitz & Co.;** Art Director/Designer: **Gloria Ruenitz;** Photography: **Pioppo & Assoc.**

To show consumers that Texas Western beef is tender, delicious and seasoned for fajitas, designer Gloria Ruenitz added see-through panels to this authentic-looking package. The red, green and yellow color palette clearly communicates that this is genuine Tex-Mex fare, while the tag line, "Fix In Six" lets consumers know that the product can be prepared quickly.

▲ **Apple Cinnamon Cheerios** for **General Mills.** Design Firm: **Hillis Mackey & Company;** Art Director/Designer/Illustrator: **Terry Mackey;** Photography: **Ed Vetsch**

General Mills wanted an entirely new look for this spin-off of the popular Cheerios breakfast cereal, a "break-through" look that would appeal to kids and adults. Hillis Mackey reached out to both market groups through carefully selected graphic elements: cereal perched on a spoon to catch the eye of adults, and a sketch of an apple, highlighted by hand-lettered type, to appeal to children. Both styles combine for a design that's both contemporary and fun.

Uncle Bum's®
Surefire Jerk Chicken and Pork

Centuries ago, the art of "jerking" was developed by the Indians of Jamaica as a method of deliciously preparing all kinds of meat for barbeque. The tasty secret was in the marinade which Uncle Bum has captured here for you. Try Uncle Bum's recipe and you'll barbeque "Jamaican style" from now on.

Perforate the meat with a fork and marinate with a generous amount of Uncle Bum's Jamaican Cooking Marinade for 1 to 24 hours. Barbeque slowly away from coals, or roast in the oven adding more marinade to keep meat moist as needed.

For extra flavor, add a little rum to the mixture. Uncle Bum's Jamaican Cooking Marinade is also great in chili, curry and any dish that needs a little extra zest.

100% Natural
No sugar, no oils, no preservatives.

**Shake well.
Refrigerate after opening.**

Ingredients: water, peppers, lime juice (from concentrate), fresh onions, soy sauce, spices, dehydrated garlic, dehydrated onions and salt.

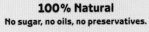

0 14733 00001 5

Bottled for Uncle Bum's Food Products, Inc.
1111 Rancho Conejo Blvd. Suite 204
Newbury Park, CA 91320 (805) 499-5449
©1986 All Rights Reserved.

❖ Marinades and Chili Sauces for **Uncle Bum's Food Products.** Art Director/Designers: **Bill Downs** (Hot Jamaican Marinade), **Laurel Shoemaker** (Seafood Marinade, right), **Wilson Ong & Sherry Johannes** (all others); Illustrators: **Chuck Murphy** (Hot Jamaican Marinade, Seafood Marinade, right), **Wilson Ong** (all others)

California-based Uncle Bum's Food Products, Inc. sells its marinades and sauces in gourmet/specialty food stores and supermarkets and in bulk to the institutional food market. All feature strong graphics and bright, bold color schemes—a deliberate attempt to distinguish these products from the competition. The newest label design for Seafood Marinade (center, left) continues the nautical theme but incorporates a colorful border made up of squares. The marlin illustration on the original seafood marinade label is repeated on the side panels—a nice touch, especially around the difficult-to-dress-up UPC code. All are printed four color with a UV varnish.

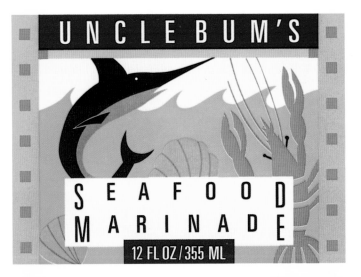

Uncle Bum's family favorite Southwestern Style Chili Sauce is a sweet pepper relish that is great for topping hamburgers, stirring into soups, stews, or rice, or as an everyday condiment, dip or spread.

©1988 Uncle Bum's Food Products, Inc.
1111 Rancho Conejo Blvd., Suite 204
Newbury Park, CA 91320 (805) 499-5449
All Rights Reserved

Uncle Bum's Romesco™ is a unique and delicious Spanish style sauce which is excellent for cooking seafood, meat, or poultry, or for using as a sauce for pasta, rice, or eggs, or as an everyday condiment or spread.

©1988 Uncle Bum's Food Products, Inc.
1111 Rancho Conejo Blvd., Suite 204
Newbury Park, CA 91320 (805) 499-5449
All Rights Reserved

▲ **Morey's Fish House** for **Morey Fish Company**. Design Firm: **Hillis Mackey & Company;** Art Director: **Jeff Hillis;** Designer: **Jim Hillis;** Illustrator: **Pete Bastiansen**

Large areas of cellophane allow the product to show through clearly, while the dark color of the tray suggests charcoal —used to smoke the fish—and icy blue suggests the fresh, clean waters of the Great Lakes.

❖ **Suzi Wan Rice** for **Uncle Ben's Inc.** Design Firm: **Kornick Lindsay;** Designers: **Kornick Lindsay staff**

Colorful bands clearly differentiate the three varieties of Suzi Wan rice dishes. Product photography showing the rice accompanied by a related entree reinforces the differentiation.

▲

❖

Canister for **Uncle Ben's Inc**. Design Firm: **Rives, Smith, Baldwin & Carlberg;** Art Director/Designer: **Sherri Oldham;** Illustrator: **Margaret Cusack**

An unusual illustration technique gives this decorative canister an authentic homespun look. Margaret Cusack stitched both a patterned background and a still life onto cloth—a technique she calls fabric collage. The collage was photographed and applied to the can by offset lithography. The center right and bottom photographs show the intricate detail of the pattern.

Microwave Rice for **MJB Rice Company.** Design Firm: **Broom & Broom, Inc.;** Art Director: **David Broom;** Designers: **David Broom, Audrey H. Hane, Kimiko Murakami Chan;** Photographer: **Pavlina Eccless**

To distinguish the first rice made especially for microwave cooking, Broom & Broom went for maximum shelf impact with large, red type and a "hero" product photo.

▲ **Breyers Yogurt** for **Kraft Dairy Group**. Design Firm: **JS Mandle & Company, Inc.;** Art Director: **James Mandle;** Designer: **Charles Flynn;** Illustrator: **Herb Reed**

Breyers' distinctive black packaging is a standout in any dairy case. Kraft asked J.S. Mandle & Company to update the image of its yogurt while retaining the enormous equity it has in its existing graphics. Large illustrations of fruit not only clearly key the flavor varieties, they also relate well to the graphics used on other Breyers products.

❖ **La Yogurt 25** for **Johanna Farms**. Design Firm: **Joel Bronz Design;** Designer: **Karen Willoughby**

This new low-calorie yogurt required a fresh approach to distinguish it from full-calorie products in the La Yogurt line and to convey a feeling of lightness and rich flavor. Printed in four color process with one match color directly onto the plastic container.

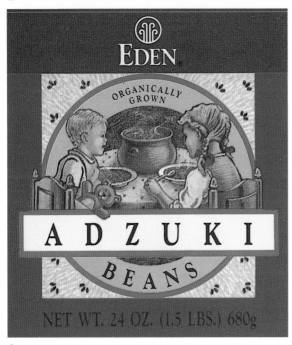

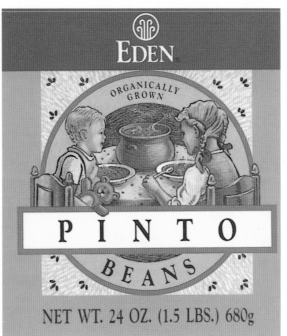

Brianna's Salad Dressing for **Del Sol Food Co**. Design Firm: **The Hively Agency;** Art Director/Designer: **Charles Hively;** Illustrators: **Bettman Archive, Dave Maloney**

These salad dressings had been on the market for several years under the Del Sol label. The name sounded Spanish even though the dressings were not. The Hively Agency suggested changing the name and redesigning the graphics. Hand-colored engravings of a single vegetable contrast nicely with the full-salad product shots used on many brands in this category.

Organic precooked beans for **Eden Foods, Inc.** Design Firm: **Perich & Partners;** Art Director/Designer: **Janine Thielk**

The graphics for this line of precooked, organically-grown beans carry a lot of freight. The homey illustrations emphasize that they are wholesome family fare. The colors were carefully coordinated with the actual color of the beans, which are packed in glass jars. Copy on the sides of the labels gives both nutritional information and intriguing recipes.

▲ Private labels and collateral materials for **Bagel Brothers Bakery & Noshery.** Design Firm: **WRK, Inc.;** Art Director/Designer/Illustrator: **Michelle Knauss**

A clever identity program and labeling system for this bakery. We especially like the illustration of two old geezers with their "bagel specs." Printed in three colors on Starliner pressure-sensitive stock.

❖ **Cycle** dog food for **The Quaker Oats Company.** Design Firm: **Peterson & Blyth;** Art Director/Designer: **David Scarlett**

An upscale look and bold brand name, set in a classic typestyle, add to Cycle's visual impact at retail. Attractive four-color photographs of canines heighten the packages' sales appeal. A numbering system and color coding differentiate the various products, which are specially formulated for the changing dietary needs of man's best friend.

■ **Miele Honey** labels for **Apistica Perugina.** Design Firm: **Packaging Design;** Art Director/Designer: **G. Italo Marchi**

Striking designs for two honey products by Italian designer G. Italo Marchi. Both feature strong horizontal patterns and symbols of a bee, but different color palettes clearly differentiate the varieties from one another.

● **Delisle Yogourt** for **Delisle Foods.** Design Firm: **Axion Design Inc.;** Art Directors: **Robert P. deVito, Kathleen Keating;** Designer: **Sharon Till;** Illustrator: **Linda Bacon**

Working your way down to the fruit at the bottom of the cup is the best part of eating yogurt. To capitalize on this culinary pleasure, Delisle Foods added the tag line "fruit on bottom" in bold script typeface. Mouthwatering illustrations of fresh fruit reinforce the sales message.

▲ **S&W Canned Vegetables** for **S&W Fine Foods, Inc.** Design Firm: **Axion Design Inc.;** Art Director: **Robert P. deVito;** Designer: **Kathleen Keating**

Little by little, major food processors and mega-conglomerates are upgrading the packaging and label graphics of their private label brands. To show customers that the foods are of comparable quality to brand name varieties, manufacturers are commissioning elaborate packaging programs and redesigns. Axion Design's effort for S&W Foods incorporates a sleek black background to show off vivid four-color photographs.

❖ **Valauris Fruit Sauce** for **E.D.G. Company.** Art Director/Designer/Illustrator: **Candice Silva**

Valauris is billed as a homemade fruit sauce based on a traditional family recipe from the Valauris region of France. The Victorian-style illustration was executed in colored pencil on Curtis Flannel stock for a soft, warm overall graphic impression. Printed four color on adhesive-back label stock.

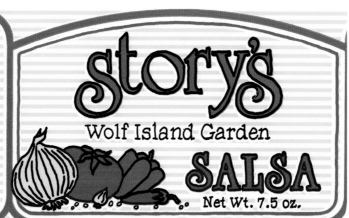

- Use as a dip or topping for chips, nachos, flautas and tortillas.
- Mix with lemon juice and horseradish for a zesty seafood sauce.
- Add to ground beef, chili beans, olives and cheese for a super Mexican dip.
- Serve with capers, olives and cheese over fish.
- Fold with Monterey Jack and butter into a tangy Mexican Omelet.
- Make a spicy addition to bean soup, chili or black eyed peas.
- Use your imagination!

If you have questions or would like additional recipes, please call toll free 1-800-345-8479.

Story's Gourmet Foods, Inc.
Wolf Island, MO 63881

Wolf Island Garden Salsa for **Story's Gourmet Foods, Inc.** Advertising Firm: **Kimwel, Inc.;** Art Director: **Sandy Richards;** Designer: **Walter Lantz;** Illustrator: **Clay Moorman;** Printer: **The Label Co.**

Kimwel, Inc. of Memphis, Tennessee, breaks from the traditional use of machine-set lettering by hand-drawing all elements of the front panel. Illustrations of fresh vegetables play on the fact that all ingredients are grown on a farm in Wolf Island, Missouri. The label is printed four color on high-gloss white Kromekote with a varnish.

● **Le Preziose Pasta** for **Buitoni.** Design Firm: **VU srl;** Art Director: **Gino Conzano;** Designer: **Gianni Parlacino;** Photography: **Perazzoli**

VU srl, an Italian packaging and marketing design studio, shows off one of Italy's greatest gifts to cuisine—pasta—by designing a oblong-shaped box with die-cut panels so consumers can see the unique shapes of the noodles. The packages are printed in six colors by offset lithography.

▲ Baby Food for **Earth's Best, Inc.** Design Firm: **American Design;** Art Director: **Allen Haeger;** Designer: **Harold Maurer;** Illustrator: **Roger Loveless**

A contemporary but still home-spun style keys the wholesome image required for this all-natural baby food.

❖ **Wax Orchards** for **Betsy Sestrap.** Design Firm: **Tim Girvin Design, Inc.;** Art Director: **Tim Girvin;** Designer: **Stephen Pannone;** Illustrator: **Anton Kimball**

A taste of tradition with a modern twist underscores the history of Wax Orchards products and highlights the natural goodness of this fruit flavoring.

▲

NO PRESERVATIVES

A delicious fresh fruit flavor for pancakes. Add *Cherry Syrup* to seltzer for a sparkling fruit drink, or to dry white wine or champagne. Make sorbets, sauces, glazes, or pour over ice cream or yogurt.
Refrigerate after opening.
Net wt. 12 fl. oz.

NO REFINED SUGAR

Pacific Northwest pie cherries, concentrated white grape, pear, peach.

For recipes & nutritional information, send S.A.S.E. to Wax Orchards, Rte. 4-320, Vashon Island, WA 98070.

❖

Seafood Poultry Sauce for **Firehouse Bar-B-Que**. Design Firm: **John Haag Design**; Art Director/Designer: **John Haag**; Illustrator: **Will Nelson**

A lemon-herb sauce for use on fish and chicken, this product is an extension to the established Firehouse Bar-B-Que line. The clean background suggests lighter fare and hints at the 1890s styling of the other Firehouse products.

Too Good Teriyaki and **Ragin' Cajun** for **DeFelice Enterprises, Inc.** Design Firm: **DeFelice Enterprises, Inc.**; Art Directors: **Vincent DeFelice, Wes Wallin**; Illustrator: **Wes Wallin**

Launching a new line of gourmet sauces requires a good product and a label that will stand out on the shelf. These bold colors are a refreshing change from the pastels and country illustrations that are so prevalent in this food category.

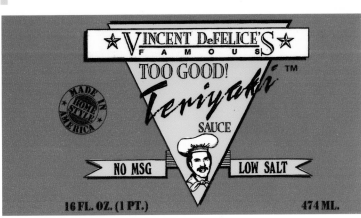

▲ **Hascup Syrup** for **Kirin Brewery**. Art Director/Designer: **Shigeru Akizuki**

A simplified print gives Hascup Syrup a traditional, agricultural feel while the paper wrap, tie cord and seal enhance the image of quality.

❖ **Avocado Oil** for **Prepco/Avoco**. Design Firm: **J. Brenlin Design**; Art Director/Designer: **Jane Brenlin**

Light, healthy and "California" were the design parameters for this oil product. The prominent illustration makes the source of the oil clear while the contemporary graphics associate it with "nouvelle" cooking.

Steak Sauce for **Heinz**. Design Firm: **Libby Perszyk Kathman;** Art Director: **Jim Henschel;** Designer/Illustrator: **Jim Gabel**

There are few names known better than Heinz. In creating a label for this traditional steak sauce, the designers had to both reflect the Heinz heritage and make a statement that is contemporary. Their task was complicated by the need to clearly set this line extension apart from the company's famous Heinz 57 brand.

Riz Cous for **Lundberg Family Farms**. Design Firm: **Image Group;** Art Director/Designer: **Jay Haws**

Cous cous is a wheat-based Moroccan dish. Riz Cous, an acronym for "rice" and "cous cous," is 100 percent natural rice. The purpose of the design was to make this all-new product feel comfortably familiar by borrowing design elements from other Lundberg packages. Each design features scans of recycled papers for the backgrounds, with texturing enhanced by colored pencil and airbrush spatters. They were produced on an Apple Macintosh design station and were printed in four-color process on 20-point SBS board.

▲ **Broadmoor Baker** bread wrapper and packaging for **Broadmoor Baker/Paul Suzman.** Design Firm: **Hornall Anderson Design Works;** Art Director: **Jack Anderson;** Designers: **Jack Anderson, Mary Hermes, Jani Drewfs;** Illustrator: **Scott McDougall**

Hornall Anderson Design Works goes beyond the standard wheat stalk design for this whole grain bread wrapper by rendering the mark in warm earthy tones—yellow, orange and blue. Copy on the side panel and a circular mark on the cellophane wrapper emphasize the product's wholesome goodness.

❖ **Dromedary Fruit Tubs** for **Specialty Brands.** Design Firm: **Walcott-Ayers & Shore;** Art Director: **Jim Walcott-Ayers;** Designers: **Jordana Welles, Jim Walcott-Ayers;** Calligrapher: **Sherry Bringham**

Originally packaged in boxes, Dromedary dried fruit was introduced in these see-through tubs as a way to expand sales. The product and logo had to be clearly visible from both the top and side, since there was no way to know how the product would be displayed in the supermarket—on a shelf, in the produce section or in a freestanding display. Hand-lettering and bright colors were chosen to illustrate the freshness and richness of the fruit. The clear plastic reusable tubs allow the consumer to judge for themselves the quality of the fruit.

■ **Marie Callendar's Croutons** for **Marie Callendar's/International Commissary Corp.** Design Firm: **Rene Yung Communications Design Inc.;** Art Director/Designer: **Rene Yung**

One look through the see-through panel on the front of the package and consumers can quickly see the home-baked goodness of these croutons. Rene Yung carries out the wholesome theme by using homey colors and a subtle pattern, which enhance both the product and the logo.

▲ Vinaigrette for **H.J. Heinz Co.** Design Firm: **Libby Perszyk Kathman;** Art Director: **Jim Henschel;** Designer: **Liz Kathman Grubow;** Illustrator: **Dianne McElwain**

For its new Red Wine and Honey Cider Vinaigrettes, H.J. Heinz asked for a look that said premium quality but which would clearly separate this new product from the existing Heinz specialty vinegars.

❖ Fruit Mince Assortment for **Big Sister**. Design Firm: **Raymond Bennett Design;** Art Director/Designer: **Raymond Bennett**

A paper wrap over the lid and bright colors key these fruit sauces by Big Sister. The labels were printed five color, allowing for a perfect color match for the company's brand mark and appetizing reproduction of the fruit illustrations.

Preserves for **Arran Provisions**. Design Firm: **Graphic Partners;** Art Director: **Ken Craig;** Designer: **Jenny Smith;** Illustrator: **Ann Ross Paterson**

The graphics for these traditional Scottish preserves, marmalades and mustards for the gourmet gift market were redesigned to position them at the high end of the market. The naive illustration and decorative style underscore the "country-made" origins of the recipes. Colors and type were used to group the products thematically within the overall line.

The junk-food frenzy that kept the snack market snapping through the '80s has abated, succeeded by a new sobriety and a return to "traditional" snack values. "All natural" and "low calorie" have lost some of their savor, the screaming "new and natural" dog ears replaced by lush visuals that say "rich, rich, rich—and *really* good."

Nowhere is this more evident than in the packaging for ice cream and frozen novelties. The calorie-and-cholesterol guilt that clouded this category seems to have dispersed somewhat. Ice creams are now being bold about how good they taste. Simplicity is the order of the day. Bold brand marks, simple background patterns and an emphasis on illustrations—rather than photographs—seem to hold sway.

As more ordinary types of food have encroached on the visual turf staked out by gourmet snack items, designers have had to evolve new ways to distinguish the higher-priced specialty foods.

Novelty containers have made a late charge. Tins, updated versions of the old cookie tin, are being used for everything from hickory chips and fruit tea to bread sticks. One of the products featured here, Story's Popcorn, comes packed in a paint bucket. The bucket has made the product very popular with kids, an interesting case where the package not only sells the product, but in a sense it *is* the product. ♦

S N A C K S

Some of the excitement has gone out of snacks as new entries have been dominated by tortilla chips and the colors of the Southwest reign. But new niches are being won with novel packaging.

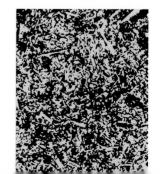

▲ **Mootown Snackers** for **Sargento Cheese**. Design Firm: **Kornick Lindsay;** Designers: **Kornick Lindsay**

The multiplicity of marketing messages required to sell Mootown Snackers had to be evident right on the front panel. The snack-sized cheeses had to look fun and inviting to children, the primary consumers, yet had to be acceptable to their parents and communicate the nutritional benefits while emphasizing convenience and portability.

❖ **Prexxels** for **Moctezuma Imports**. Design Firm: **Jamie Davison Design, Inc.;** Art Director/ Designer: **Jamie Davison;** Photographer: **Richard Eskite**

Cerveceria Moctezuma of Mexico produces Dos Equis beer and these pretzels. The package had to preserve and reinforce the Dos Equis identity, which is well established in the United States. It also had to convey the rich, buttery flavor of the snacks.

▲

❖

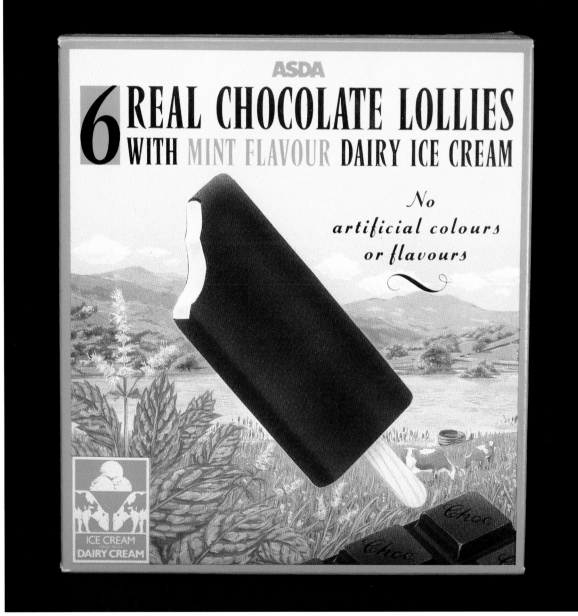

ASDA

6 REAL CHOCOLATE LOLLIES
WITH MINT FLAVOUR DAIRY ICE CREAM

No artificial colours or flavours

ICE CREAM
DAIRY CREAM

■ **Gervais** for **Findus**. Design Firm: **Design Board Behaegel & Partners;** Art Director: **Denis Keller;** Designers/Illustrators: **Erik Vantal, Christina Jans**

Primary colors and a central illustration help these new Gervais novelties project from the frozen foods case.

● **Well Done Potato Chips**. Design Firm: **The Design Company;** Designers: **The Design Company**

Potato snacks literally throng the shelves of supermarkets, convenience stores, even drugstores. This new product needed a bright, bold label that would draw attention to its difference: potato chips that have been cooked a little beyond medium rare.

☆ Chocolate Ice Cream Novelties for **Asda Stores, Ltd**. Design Firm: **Elmwood Design, Ltd;** Designer: **Clare Walker;** Illustrator: **Ken Binder**

The lush rendering on the label for these confections is very different from the neon colors and airbrush style often used on frozen novelties. The scene says purity and goodness, desirable attributes in any milk product.

▲ Cake box for **Just Desserts.** Design Firm: **Primo Angeli Inc.;** Creative Director: **Primo Angeli;** Designers: **Phillipe Becker, Ray Honda, Primo Angeli**

When Primo Angeli Inc. created the original imagery for Just Desserts, a purveyor of baked goods in San Francisco, the company was small, but hip. As the bakery grew, its customer base became more varied and more wealthy. This redesign retains the original mark, but adds just the right amount of sophistication.

❖ Wafer Cones for **Elite Ltd**. Design Firm: **Vardimon/Adler Studios** Art Director/Designer: **Yarom Vardimon;** Illustrator: **Moshe Alenbic**

This festive packaging for ice cream cones and cups is printed in five colors on coated board stock.

▲

❖

Packaging for **Ethel-M Choco-
lates**. Design Firm: **Bright &
Associates**; Art Director: **Keith
Bright;** Designer/Illustrator:
Ray Wood

Ethel-M needed imagery which
could be applied to a wide variety of package sizes and
shapes for its many confections. A silver symbol—which
can be combined with boxes of
different sizes and colors and
with ribbons and hang tags—is
an elegantly simple solution.

▲ **Fruit Ripples** for **Stretch Is-land Fruit, Inc**. Design Firm: **American Design;** Art Director: **Allen Haeger;** Designer/Illustrator: **Roger Gefvert**

Fruit products and tropical imagery seem to be inseparable. While the vernacular here—palm trees, vibrant colors and birds—is familiar ground, the quality of the illustrations, central billboard and type combine to create a memorable effect.

❖ **Kuzuka** for **Souhonke Suru-gaya**. Design Firm: **Maeda Design Associates;** Art Director/Designer: **Kazuki Maeda**

Traditional Japanese sweets for the summer season are served up in an impressive style. The fruits are packed in individual plastic bags containing syrup, then dressed up with a hang tag and ribbon.

▲

❖

Effie Marie's Rum Butter Cakes for **Heritage Kitchens**. Design Firm: **SBG Partners;** Art Director: **Nicholas Sidjakov;** Designer: **Barbara Vick;** Illustrator: **Carolyn Vibbert**

We've come a long way from Twinkies. Today, Victoriana reigns supreme in the baked goods section, where gourmet confections of every variety have flooded the market. Heritage Kitchens asked SBG Partners to redesign its well-known Effie Marie packaging to bolster share in an increasingly competitive category.

● **Teenee Beanees** for **Just Born**. Design Firm: **Peterson & Blyth;** Art Director: **John Blyth;** Designer: **Jacquie Fauter-MacConnell;** Illustrator: **Robert Evans**

What's the difference between candy store jelly beans and gourmet jelly beans? Well, for one thing, your garden-variety bean doesn't come in an elegant package like these. The image adds value and increases the product's appeal to young adults who still have a sweet tooth—and now have the salary to support it.

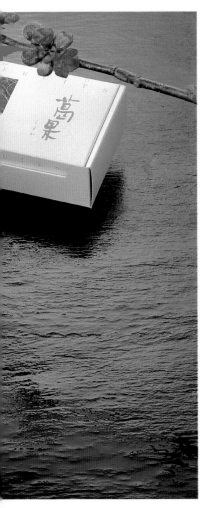

▲ Candy bar for **Health Rich**. Design Firm: **American Design**; Art Director: **Allen Haeger**; Designer: **Jill Finche-Graham**

The ingredients for this candy bar are not only "natural," they're certified organic: grown without herbicides, pesticides or synthetic fertilizers. The typographic treatment emphasizes this while the bright colors were intended to create a festive look that would appeal to children and adults with a sweet tooth.

❖ **Cornuts Asian Exports** for **Cornuts, Inc.** Design Firm: **The Thompson Design Group**; Art Director: **Dennis Thompson**; Designer: **Veronica Denny**

To introduce its corn-based snack to markets in Asia, Cornuts asked for a vibrant package that would compete visually with the colorful packaging found in Asian food stores and show off the product. Thompson Design used five colors plus varnish on metallized foil to reproduce an airbrushed background and an illustration of the product in both its raw and finished state.

▲

❖

■ **Arare Rice Puffs** for **Eden Foods, Inc**. Design Firm: **Eden Foods, Inc.** Designers: **Eden Foods staff**

Arare snacks are an ancient and familiar food in Japan, but were introduced to the U.S. only recently. Brown rice is cooked, then pounded into a dough which is baked until crispy. The striking bird illustration carries the Eden Foods logo, which itself suggests stalks of grain. The result is a package which looks about as different from Doritos and Ritz Crackers as you can get. Copy on the back of the package describes the history and composition of the product.

▲ Wafers for **Elite Ltd.** Design Firm: **Vardimon/Adler Studios;** Art Director/Designer: **Yarom Vardimon;** Illustrator: **Michel Kishka**

Bright colors and a botanical-style illustration of hazelnuts spark this bright packaging for sugar wafers.

❖ Chocolates for **Richard H. Donnelly.** Design Firm: **Colonna, Farrell: Strategic Marketing & Design;** Art Directors: **Ralph Colonna, Richard Clark;** Designers: **Susan Handly, Amy Racina**

European confectioner Richard Donnelly asked for a complete identity program for his handmade line of chocolates. The premium sweets are intended as gifts. White Kromekote and Black Vista Gloss papers gave the design the depth of finish while gold foil embossing supports the ritzy logo treatment.

▲

❖

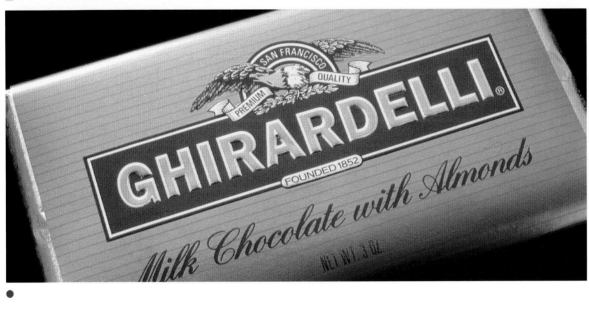

■ Chocolate chips for **Guittard Chocolate Company**. Design Firm: **The Thompson Design Group;** Art Director: **Dennis Thompson;** Designer: **Veronica Denny**

A proprietary type treatment and gold foil help convey the premium positioning for these chocolate chip bits. The product is opened for the buyer's inspection by means of a small transparent area beneath the main label.

● Chocolate bar for **Ghirardelli Chocolate Company**. Design Firm: **SBG Partners;** Art Director: **Nicholas Sidjakov;** Designer: **Dave Curtis**

Detroit has its "Big Three" and the world of fine chocolates has its "Big Gs:" Godiva and Ghirardelli. This label squeezes every last ounce of juice out of Ghirardelli's long and notable tradition. The rich foil, the eagle and scroll and the "hero" type treatment all say that this bar is, in fact, the very best.

▲ **MIke and Ike, Hot Tamales, Jolly Joes** for **Just Born**. Design Firm: **Peterson & Blyth**; Art Director: **John S. Blyth**; Designers: **Peterson & Blyth**

Color is the name of the game at the candy counter. Peterson & Blyth's packages for Just Born provide it in a big way, with the products strewn confetti-like all over the boxes.

❖ **Weight Watchers Grand Ice Milk Collection** for **H.J. Heinz Co.** Design Firm: **Libby Perszyk Kathman**; Art Director: **Jim Henschel**; Designer: **John Metz**; Photographer: **Peter Pioppo**

An ice cream for folks on a diet? Of course—Weight Watchers provides everything the hungry but calorie-conscious could want. Libby Perszyk Kathman's job was to develop a unique identity for these ice milks within the overall Weight Watchers line and to project richness and flavor.

While these five products were not new, Dil Publicidade brought them together under a single brand name, Frizz, and gave them a unified graphic identity. The continuous-flow machinery used to pack the liquid product required that the label be repeated twice on each of the pops.

The task was to make the graphics for Drake Bakeries' line of snacks more contemporary without getting overly futuristic. The designers felt that too futuristic a look would give buyer's a negative perception of the ingredients of these traditional confections.

▲ **Nectar Nuggets** for **Natural Nectar**. Design Firm: **Harte Yamashita & Forest;** Art Director/Designer: **Denise Georgeson;** Illustrators: **Will Nelson, David Scanlon**

Six colors—four applied by rotogravure and two by flexography—on metallic foil create an intensely colorful, neon-like effect that makes Nectar Nuggets all-natural candies a stand-out in any candy section.

❖ Ice cream for **Leopardi**. Design Firm: **Michael Peters + Partners;** Art Director/Designer: **Glenn Tutssel;** Illustrators: **Liz Pyle, Roy Knipe**

A rich, "real Italian" look was achieved for this full-calorie ice cream made for sale in the United Kingdom. Ribbons, soft pastel colors, illustrations of flavor ingredients and a happy Italian couple give the package a complex, yet visually soft texture. Unusual copy placement draws attention to a quote from the creator of Leopardi.

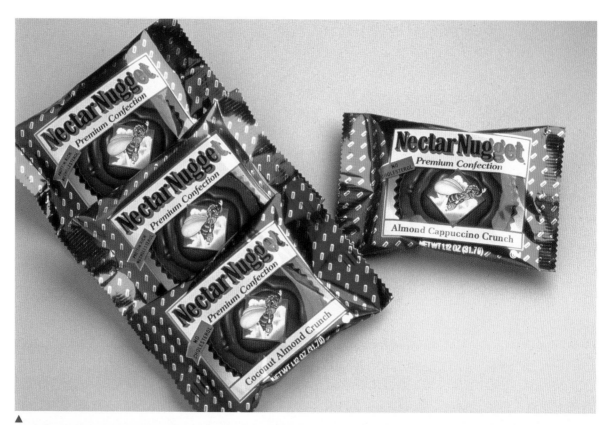

▲

❖

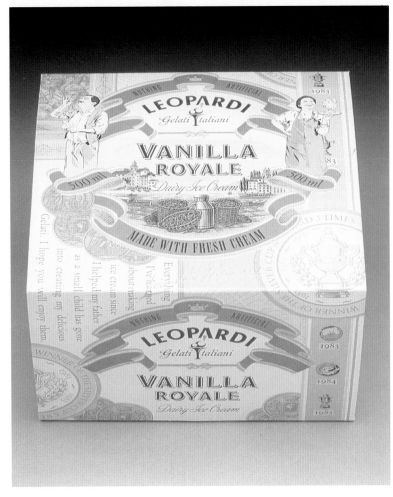

Petit Cœurs for **Fleischmann & Royal**. Design Firm: **Dil Publicidade, Ltda;** Designers: **Dil Publicidade staff**

A special Christmas package for chocolate and cinnamon cookies, this box of Petit Cœurs is designed as a gift. A winter landscape on the front is accompanied by a legend on the back panel which attributes the recipe for the cookies to the mythical gnomes that inhabit meadows in France.

▲ **Almond Brittle** and **Rocky Pop** for **Rocky Mountain Chocolate Factory.** Design Firm: **Image Group, Inc.;** Art Director/Designer/Illustrator: **Jay Haws**

Commonly located in high-traffic tourist areas, Rocky Mountain Chocolate Factory franchise stores produce Rocky Pop and five specialty nut brittles on the premises. The fresh candy is sold as a gourmet snack for immediate consumption and as a fun take-home treat. The label design visually communicates a nostalgic image reminiscent of a hand-tinted engraving to emphasize the message of old-fashioned goodness.

❖ **Fi·bar Chewy & Nutty** for **Natural Nectar.** Design Firm: **Harte Yamashita & Forest;** Art Director: **Susan Healy;** Designers: **Susan Healy, Denise Georgeson;** Photographer: **Henry Bjoin**

Building on the equity of the original Fi•bar graphics program it developed, Harte Yamashita & Forest relied on vibrant colors and bold graphic elements to appeal to a young audience. The packages are printed in six colors with a varnish by offset lithography.

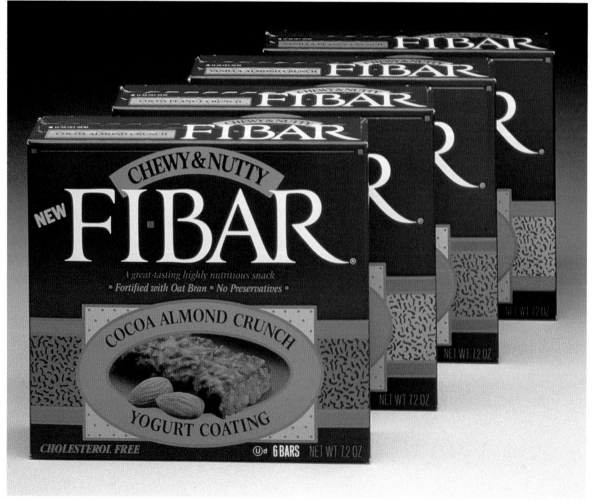

■ **Drake's Pick♥M♥Ups** for **Drake Bakeries.** Design Firm: **The Berni Company;** Art Director: **Stuart M. Berni, FPDC;** Designer: **Jung Kim;** Photographer: **Steven Stuart**

Mouth-watering four-color photographs and a highly-stylized logo position these frozen baked goods as fresh and delicious, comparable in quality to higher-priced frozen baked goods and freshly-baked treats.

● **"Quést-ce que" confections** for **Souhonke Surugaya.** Design Firm: **Maeda Design Associates;** Art Director/Designer: **Kazuki Maeda**

Designer Kazuki Maeda takes a contemporary approach to the Japanese tradition of wrapping candies in tiny gift packages with various types of Japanese papers in trendy colors.

▲ **Frozen Yogurt** for **Great American Foods**. Design Firm: **The Weller Institute for the Cure of Design, Inc.;** Art Directors: **Don Weller, Kevin Sheehan;** Designer/Illustrator: **Don Weller**

Light, friendly and fun were the prerequisites for Great American Foods' frozen yogurt mix. The colors suggest ice cream while the cow points out the fact that yogurt is a dairy food, too.

❖ **Borden Frozen Yogurt** for **Borden Dairy Group.** Design Firm: **Kornick Lindsay;** Illustrator: **Steven Edsey**

Although well-known as a purveyor of ice cream, this is Borden's first foray into the frozen yogurt category. Kornick Lindsay was asked to incorporate the company's existing brand equities into the package, create a design that could be extended to additional products in the future and establish a premium-quality position for the brand.

■ **Kemps Frozen Yogurt** for **Marigold Foods**. Design Firm: **Hillis Mackey & Company;** Art Directors: **Barbara Hauger, Jim Hillis;** Designers: **Jim Hillis, Barbara Hauger;** Illustrator: **Kate Brennan Hall**

Using a stylized illustration of fruit as its central focus allowed Hillis Mackey to create a package that is easily printed by flexography, keeping costs at a minimum for this can-style container. The white background and green grid keep the look light and airy.

● **Kemps Frozen Custard** for **Marigold Foods.** Design Firm: **Hillis Mackey & Company;** Art Director/Designer: **Terry Mackey;** Illustrator: **Kate Brennan Hall;** Lettering: **Bill Kroll**

Unlike yogurt, frozen custard is a full-calorie product, and Marigold Foods asked for a rich feeling for its Kemps custard. Saturated colors and a woodcut-style illustration of milk and eggs appeal to the health conscious while still giving the impression that the custard is just a bit indulgent.

▲ **Flav-O-Rich** for **Dairymen.** Design Firm: **Peterson & Blyth;** Art Director: **David Scarlett;** Designers: **Peterson & Blyth**

The bright colors of the ice cream treats really stand out against the black background selected for this packaging. Reversing out the brand name in white strengthens the overall presentation.

❖ **Popcorn** for **Story's Gourmet Foods, Inc.** Design Firm: **Lane/ Mazzone & Associates;** Designers: **Ray Lane, Darlene Mazzone, Jaime McPherson, Jill Miller;** Artist: **Cyd Moore**

Popcorn merchandised in a bucket? The idea started with owner Lee Story, who thought that paint cans would make unique containers. Designers at Lane/Mazzone & Associates took the concept further and developed Story's Fun Bucket and Designer Pail. The designers reasoned that even though the popcorn is of the very highest quality, what would really sell the product to women and children—the two target markets—would be an eye-catching design and the fact the can be used as a bucket after it's emptied. This whimsical package comes with a coloring book and crayons. A triangular-shaped hang tag alerts consumers to the free gift inside. The labels are large: 7¼" x 21½", and are printed flat, with two die-cut circles, in four colors on 70-pound C1S Simpson stock.

■ **Nestlé** ice cream bars for **Nestlé Foods.** Design Firm: **Hans Flink Design Inc.;** Art Directors: **Hans D. Flink, Ron Vandenberg;** Designers: **Hans Flink Design**

New packaging for the Nestlé ice cream bar is simple and direct. The design avoids any suggestion of premium price, bolstering the product's position as a quality treat for every day consumption. Printed in four colors.

▲ **Plum Pudding** label for **Big Sister.** Design Firm: **Raymond Bennett Design;** Art Director/Designer: **Raymond Bennett**

A rich looking label for a rich dessert product. Australian designer Raymond Bennett creates a classic look of dark hues and four-color photography.

❖ **Self-Saucing Pudding** for **Big Sister.** Design Firm: **Raymond Bennett Design;** Art Director/Designer: **Raymond Bennett**

Large product photos make it easy to discern both the flavor and the "self-saucing" feature of these canned puddings. Color coding helps differentiate these items while the graphic treatment is consistent with the large range of Big Sister dessert and snack items.

■ Assorted fruit cakes for **Big Sister.** Design Firm: **Raymond Bennett Design;** Art Director/Designer: **Raymond Bennett**

The foil paper and the oil-fashioned script typestyle make these packages look as rich and elegant as the cakes inside. The graphics and materials are a radical departure from Bennett's other designs for Big Sister.

▲

❖

■

● **Pik-Nik Shoestring Potatoes** for **S&W Fine Foods, Inc.** Design Firm: **Axion Design Inc.;** Art Director: **Kathleen Keating;** Designer: **Eric Read;** Illustrator: **Linda Bacon**

This old-fashioned package design for Pik-Nik Shoestring Potatoes not only demonstrates the emphasis that S&W Fine Foods puts on excellent design, but the versatility of its design firm, Axion Design Inc. The California firm has created a lot of different looks for S&W Fine Foods. A colorful illustration of picnic foods spread out on a checkered blanket conjures up fond memories of picnicking on a warm summer day.

BEVERAGES

Beverages have come into their own as a design category. Once the near-exclusive turf of the cola giants, broadening consumer tastes have allowed in not only new brands but new kinds of thirst-quenchers. Juice-based products continue their ascendancy and the bright colors associated with them have become a seemingly permanent fixture on the design scene.

And while much of the rest of the design world has moved on, Post-Modernism seems to have found a niche in the beverage aisle. As one wag put it, "you know, shapes floating all over and if you don't know what to do, tear the paper." The saturated colors favored for the category harmonize well with hard geometric shapes, so this may be a vocabulary that lasts for a while. Just as we now think of expensive chocolate bars and script type as a natural pair, funky typefaces set at an angle may be the most obvious complement to a new-and-different beverage.

The emphasis on fruit and natural ingredients has also encouraged the use of botanical-style illustrations with, in some cases, more classic typeforms and styling.

As the supply of underexploited fruit flavorings is virtually inexhaustible and the consumer desire for more—and more exotic—drinks seems likewise limitless, look for beverages to remain a frontier for both marketers and designers. ♦

Once a virtual design desert, the beverage bar is now a visual cornucopia, flowing with "natural goodness" and jumping with Post-Modern geometrics.

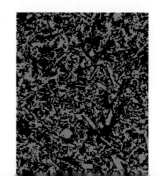

▲ **Blue Roo** soft drink for **Blue Roo.** Design Firm: **Stan Evenson Design;** Art Director/Designer: **Stan Evenson;** Illustrator: **Byron Gin**

This Australian soft drink needed a bold but friendly label. The blue kangaroo is a uniquely Australian symbol.

❖ **Looza** juices for **Looza.** Design Firm: **Design Board Behaeghel & Partners;** Art Director: **Denis Keller;** Designer/Illustrator: **Johan Corvers**

Looza is a leading pure juice drink manufacturer in Belgium. Among the elements of this new identity program is a bold logo reversed out of a brilliant red background.

■ **Sparkling Water** for **Tiger Alley Restaurant.** Design Firm: **Gerald Reis & Company;** Art Director: **Gerald Reis;** Designers: **Gerald Reis, Albert Treskin, John Malmquist**

This label, and its companion wine label, is refined in concept but suggests a scrappy, playful imagery. As the interior of the restaurant is quite formal, the designers relied on graphic elements to convey elegance without being overly serious.

▲ **Lavazza Coffee**. Design Firm: **Primo Angeli Inc.;** Creative Director: **Primo Angeli;** Designers: **Primo Angeli, Ian McLean, Mark Crumpacker, Rolando Rosler**

Lavazza has been selling coffee in Italy for over a century. Before introducing the brand in America, the company sought to create a unified look for its varied product line. Its research showed that Americans weren't happy with the way their coffee tasted. To capitalize on that, Lavazza wanted to portray the Italian attitude toward coffee—that it is more than a beverage, it is part of a lifestyle—in its new graphics.

▲

❖ **Superior Coffee** for **Superior Coffee & Foods**. Design Firm: **Kornick Lindsay;** Designers: **Kornick Lindsay**

For its gourmet/premium coffee beans, Superior sought a visual identity which would underscore the quality of the products and reorganize the varieties into families for clear visual communication. The labels are offset on foil while the bags are printed by flexographic offset. In addition to its graphic qualities, the new packaging reduced Superior's cost of manufacturing.

▲ Self-promotional holiday gift. Design Firm: **Image Group, Inc.;** Art Director/Designer: **Suzanne Bastear;** Illustrator: **David Zavala;** Lithography: **Walker Lithograph, Tom Walker;** Film Preparation: **Summerfield Graphics**

As a seasonal gift for its clients, Image Group designed a special label for packages of Brothers' Coffee. The labels were printed four-color process plus gloss varnish on self-adhesive stock. A matching card was designed to accompany the gift.

❖ **Il Classico** for **S&W Fine Foods, Inc.** Design Firm: **Axion Design Inc.;** Art Directors: **Robert P. deVito, Kathleen Keating;** Designer: **Lisa Brussell**

The rich flavor of Italian-style espresso is represented by saturated colors and traditional images: a view of a Venetian canal, a bust of the Roman god Janus and rococo embellishments.

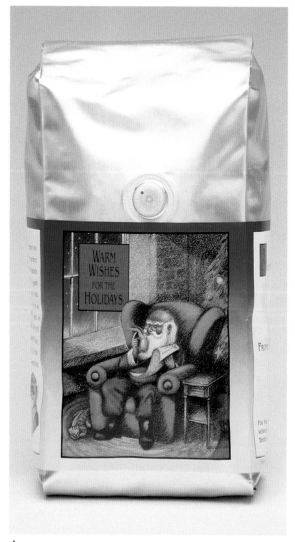

Finley Ltd. Coffee for **Superior Coffee & Foods**. Design Firm: **Kornick Lindsay;** Designers: **Kornick Lindsay**

Finley Ltd., a division of Superior Coffee, wanted a richer and more uniform presentation for its line of gourmet coffee beans. Flexible-film bags printed by flexographic offset and offset foil labels were an economical and visually appealing choice.

● **Brothers' Coffee**. Design Firm: **Image Group, Inc.;** Art Director/Designer: **Suzanne Bastear;** Illustrator: **Deborah Cunninghame-Blank**

The colorful, Impressionist-style pastel rendering was created for the initial mock-up, but it had such spontaneity and impact that it was used as the final art. The soft, warm look is a departure from the gold foil and earth tones often selected for coffee packaging.

▲ Tea containers for **Liverpool-Shanghai Tea Co., Ltd**. Design Firm: **Alan Chan Design Company;** Art Director: **Alan Chan;** Designers: **Alan Chan, Alvin Chan, Phillip Leung**

Featuring historic Chinese scenes and symbols, the containers featured on these two pages were designed for a broad selection of high-quality Chinese and Taiwanese teas.

▲ **Chiquita Orange Banana Juice** for **Chiquita Brands**. Design Firm: **The Berni Company**; Art Director: **Stephen H. Berni**; Designer: **Mark Eckstein**

Long a household word in connection with fruit, when Chiquita began marketing juice products, it asked for an image that would both play on the equity of the Chiquita name and support the high expectations consumers have for products sold under the Chiquita brand.

❖ **Minute Maid Juices** for **Coca-Cola Foods**. Design Firm: **Kornick Lindsay**; Designers: **Kornick Lindsay**

Minute Maid is another well-known brand. A sleek, orange pitcher-style container was paired with uncluttered, straightforward graphics for its concentrate product, while a white container and a photograph of a fresh, whole orange pitches the more expensive Premium fresh-squeezed juice to shoppers who are less price-conscious.

▪ **Crystal Geyser Juice Squeeze** for **Crystal Geyser Water Co**. Design Firm: **Colonna, Farrell: Strategic Marketing & Design**; Art Director: **Ralph Colonna**; Designers: **Cynthia Maguire, Peggy Koch**; Illustrator: **Beth Whybrow Leeds**; Printer: **H.S. Crocker**

Not a "natural soda" or a "juice-blend product," the message given by the graphics is clear: All natural juice with a dash of mineral water. Printed on 60-pound Simpson C1S.

▲

❖

▲ Soft drinks for **Barraclough's Soft Drinks**. Design Firm: **Elmwood Design Ltd.;** Designers: **Christine Towler, Julia White;** Illustrators: **J. Richardson, Ken Binder, Gill Marklew**

Botanical illustrations and soft, natural colors help say that Barraclough's range of traditional-style soft drinks are made the old-fashioned way.

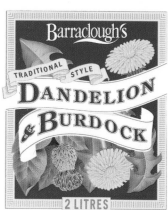

❖ Juices for **California Groves**. Design Firm: **Colonna, Farrell: Strategic Marketing & Design**; Art Director: **Ralph Colonna**; Designer: **Amy Racina**; Illustrator: **Mike Gray**

It's a given that fruit juice packaging uses illustrations of fruit and bright colors. But here, Colonna, Farrell has let the natural color of the juices—diffused through a translucent plastic jug—provide the background while bold type spells out the varieties.

■ **Tacc Lima** for **Bols Argentina, S.A**. Design Firm: **Estudio Hache**; Designers: **Marcelo Varela, Laura Lazzeretti**

Here, clear glass shows off the product while bright graphics draw attention to the brand name and label copy.

● **Lite Line Milk** for **Borden Dairy Group**. Design Firm: **Kornick Lindsay**; Designers: **Kornick Lindsay**

Borden's trademark, Elsie the cow, gets a whole new look in this package for Lite Line, the dairy's reduced-fat milk. The white background, rather than the red and purple favored for milk products, gives the carton a visual advantage in the dairy case.

▲ **Europa** for **Europa Products, Inc.** Design Firm: **The Thompson Design Group;** Art Directors: **Dennis Thompson, Jody Thompson;** Designers: **Dennis Thompson, Elizabeth Berta**

Thompson Design promotes the European origin of these fruit juice and sparkling water beverages with an authentic product name—Europa—and colorful splash graphics. The label and neck band are printed in three colors with a varnish; the cap is printed in two colors.

❖ **Hot Cocoa Mix** for **Hills Bros. Coffee, Inc.** Design Firm: **Broom & Broom, Inc.;** Art Director: **David Broom;** Designers: **David Broom, Kimiko Murakami Chan;** Photographer: **Brad Chaney**

Hot cocoa has been a cold weather staple for years. This redesign seeks to convey quality and appeal to a younger audience. Printed five colors with a varnish on solid bleach board stock.

▲

❖

■ **Maxwell House Coffee** for **Maxwell House Coffee Company.** Design Firm: **Landor Associates;** Art Directors: **Daniel Andrist, Jack Vogler;** Designers: **Jonathan Weden, Carlos Seminario**

In updating the look of perhaps the most recognizable brand of coffee, Landor Associates retains the equities of the old packaging and communicates, through a colorful rendition of the "Good to the Last Drop" brand mark, that this is a quality coffee—both instant and regular. Printed in six colors.

● **Nestea** for **Nestlé Foods.** Design Firm: **Hans Flink Design Inc.;** Art Directors: **Hans D. Flink, Ron Vandenberg;** Designers: **Hans D. Flink Design**

Nestlé Foods takes the plunge with bold graphics for its Nestea pre-mixed iced tea. The old package design (left) looked dated. To project a more contemporary image, Hans Flink Design relied on a poster-style illustration and diagonal layout to enhance shelf impact. Printed in four colors by lithography.

▲ **Maxwell House Rich French Roast** for **Maxwell House Coffee Company**. Design Firm: **Landor Associates, New York** Art Director: **Karen Corell;** Designer: **Carlos Seminario**

The visual identity for Maxwell House French Roast Coffee had to be distinctive and inviting, but still fit into the revised graphic scheme for all Maxwell House brands.

❖ **Hills Gold Coffee** for **Hills Brothers Coffee, Inc.** Design Firm: **The Thompson Design Group;** Art Directors: **Dennis Thompson, Jody Thompson;** Designers: **Dennis Thompson, Elizabeth Berta;** Illustrator: **Elizabeth Berta**

To promote the package's use as a decorative canister, a straight-wall container was used in place of the more common beaded-wall canister. The graphics were printed in four colors with gold ink and a matte varnish.

■ **Fong Ming Tong Tea Leaves** for **Liverpool-Shanghai Tea Co., Ltd**. Design Firm: **Alan Chan Design Company;** Art Director: **Alan Chan;** Designers: **Alan Chan, Alvin Chan, Phillip Leung**

Designed for high-quality Chinese and Taiwanese teas, the image of a scholar riding a dragon is taken from Chinese folklore.

▲ **Chaudfontaine** for **Piedboeuf.**
Design Firm: **Design Board Behaeghel & Partners;** Art Director: **Denis Keller;** Designer/Illus-
trator: **Erik Vantal**

Light blue—a cool color—and
cherry red—a warm color—combine with a transparent package
to illustrate the lightness and purity of this bottled water.

❖ **Faygo soft drinks** for **Faygo
Beverages, Inc.** Design Firm:
Primo Angeli Inc. Creative Director: **Primo Angeli;** Designers: **Vicki Cero, Terrence Tong**

A large U.S. bottler of carbonat-
ed beverages based in Detroit,
Faygo asked for a new identity
program that would enhance
consumer recognition of its large
line of flavored soft drinks. The
graphics focus attention on the
fruits used to flavor the drinks
and are designed to make a distinctive mass display.

▲

❖

Vogue Soft Drinks and **Lemonade** for **G. Barracloughs Ltd.** Design Firm: **Elmwood Design Ltd.;** Designer: **Clare Walker;** Illustrator: **Gill Marklew**

Trendy graphics seem appropriate for a product named Vogue. Clever tag lines and copy blocks are particularly appealing to the target audience—teenagers.

▲ **Schoon Spruit** for **Beechams South Africa.** Design Firm: **Pentagraph;** Designers: **Pentagraph Design Team**

While juices, coolers and sodas are often packaged in a wild variety of bright colors, bottled water demands a low-key approach. The message that Schoon Spruit is refreshing is carried by clear tones of light blue and an illustration of a snow-capped mountain.

Lincoln Juices for **Sundor Brands**. Design Firm: **The Berni Company**; Art Director: **Stuart M. Berni FPDC**; Designer: **Jung Kim**; Illustrator: **Gary Chicarelli**

A welter of confusing sub-brand identities were fused into a coherent, brand-wide labeling system for Sundor's Lincoln juices. Color variations were used to distinguish the various types of juice products.

Speas Farm Juice for **Sundor Brands**. Design Firm: **The Berni Company**; Art Director: **Mark Eckstein**; Designer: **Louis Romita**; Illustrator: **Will Nelson**

The proliferation of juice product varieties led Sundor to seek a unified look for its widely-distributed Speas Farm brand. The new labels were designed to give Speas Farm a boost in new categories in which Sundor felt it had the greatest leverage.

☆ **Oolong Tea** for **K.C.B. Foods Service Corporation**. Design Firm: **Maeda Design Associates**; Art Director: **Kazuki Maeda**; Designer: **Kenichi Tawarazumita**; Illustrator: **Seiichi Maeda**

This can looks cool and frosty even when it's not. The white tint applied to the aluminum gives the viewer the impression of coolness, while the flavor variety is clearly spelled out in both ideograms and in English.

▲ **Coffee** for **Consilia.** Design Firm: **Michael Peters + Partners;** Art Director/Designer: **Pat Perchal;** Illustrator: **Harry Willock**

Diehard coffee drinkers are passionate about their beans, and equally particular about the packaging. It must depict the uniqueness of the bean and capture the rich taste and deep aroma of a superb brew. This package design does all this and more—from the gold foil stamping to the deep, rich hues. Printed via gravure.

❖ **Orange juice** for **Goodmans.** Design Firm: **Michael Peters + Partners;** Art Director: **Glenn Tutssel;** Designer: **David Beard;** Illustrator: **Rory Kee**

The upright cardboard container featured on the opposite page looks like a carton for a fine wine, but in this case it contains fresh orange juice (see bottom photo this page). The mouth-watering graphics tell the whole story. Self-adhesive labels on the bottles inside were produced on a letterpress; the box was printed via lithography.

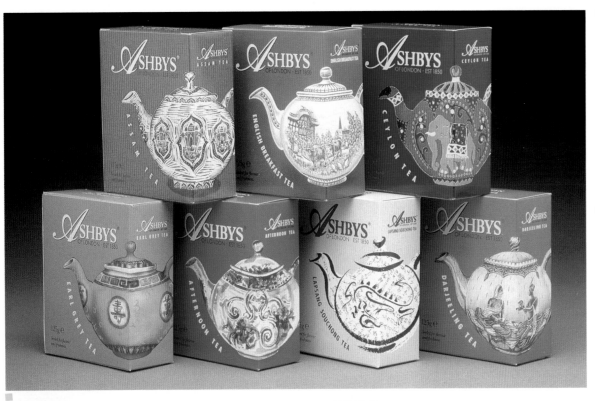

Soda Water

Tea for **Ashby's.** Design Firm: **Michael Peters + Partners;** Art Director: **Mark Pearce;** Designer: **Sherine Raouf**

Each box features an illustration representing the country of origin. For instance, a view of the English countryside adorns the English Breakfast Tea box, while Japanese symbols can be found on the Earl Grey Tea packaging. Boxes are printed by lithography.

Soft drinks for **Villa Soft Drinks.** Design Firm: **Elmwood Design Ltd.;** Designers: **Clare Walker, Karen Ellis**

Villa has been producing soft drinks for more than a century. This design seeks to enhance the company's traditional image in a refreshing way. The dots represent the carbonation.

▲ **Natural Juices** for **Organic Farms.** Design Firm: **American Design;** Art Director: **Allen Haeger;** Designer: **Harold Maurer;** Illustrator: **Mark Stutzman**

You'll find some of the most attractive labels in the beverage section of natural and gourmet stores, as evidenced by this classy design by American Design. A clean, simplistic illustration serves as the focal point, and is highlighted by the product name in a script typeface. A subtle background of monochromatic colors completes the sophisticated look.

❖ **Go Nectar** for **Star.** Design Firm: **VU srl;** Art Director: **Gianni Parlacino;** Designer: **Annalisa Papa;** Illustrators: **Walter Di Pino, Pierluigi Gatto**

This is a fun design, and we especially like the product name. The designers incorporated a lot of interesting elements—a playful typeface, whimsical illustrations and bright, eye-catching colors.

■ **Organic Original Edensoy** for **Eden Foods, Inc.** Design Firm: **Perich & Partners;** Art Director/Designer: **Janine Thielk;** Printer: **Tetra Pak, Inc.**

Not many clients are adventurous enough to feature a watercolor-like illustration on the front of a beverage package. Eden Foods is, and the results have been positive. The Clinton, Michigan company wanted a package that positions Eden-Soy as a unique beverage (it's made from soybeans and barley) without imitating the look of either milk cartons or juice containers. A bright yellow seal on the front and magenta-color copy emphasize the natural ingredients. Printed in five colors.

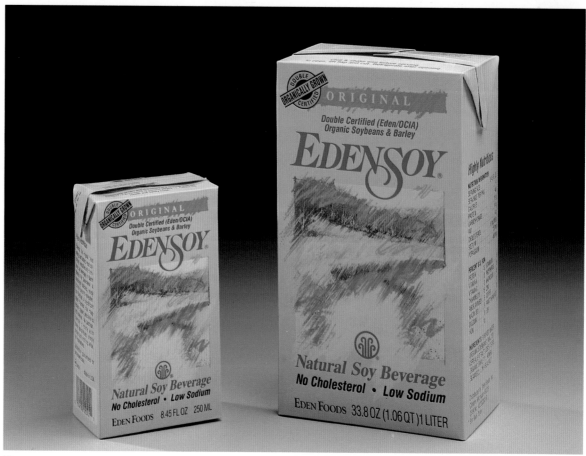

● **Mariana** for **Delhaize.** Design Firm: **Design Board Behaeghel & Partners;** Art Director: **Denis Keller;** Designer/Illustrator: **Sally Swart**

Mariana is a "light" coffee that contains less caffeine than de-caffeinated coffee. An Impressionistic-style illustration shows two young people enjoying the full-bodied brew.

☆ **Creativitea,** a self-promotional tea for **Butler Kosh Brooks.** Art Director: **Butler Kosh Brooks;** Printer: **Welsh Graphics;** Ink: **Ink Systems Inc.**

Creativitea was sent to existing and prospective clients to solicit more packaging work. Printed in six colors; ink sequence: Red-yellow-cyan-black.

WINE

American wines—and American wineries—seem to have staged a coup of sorts. With the California complement in the van, the bold, non-traditional approach to wine label design begun here a decade ago has reached full flower. In the Americas, at least, traditional designs are becoming the exception, rather than the rule. And that boldness seems to have reached across the ocean and echoed back. Around the Pacific Rim, designers have seized on the freedom of expression pioneered by iconoclastic California vintners to make their own individualized statements. As California design firms have become more active in designing labels for European wineries, their style is seen more often there, too.

As a philosophy, Post-Modernism has struck a responsive chord in the wine market. Given the limitless number of wines, the eccentricity and emphasis on individuality that underlie Post-Modernism provide ample latitude for designers to express the personality of the wine or the winemaker.

A more sophisticated and restrained style is emerging as well. Many of the stylistic elements which have become common in graphics used for foods, snacks, beverages and even consumer goods were borrowed from wine labels. Borders, background patterns, small type and color shading are being used more often and with greater subtlety. ♦

Californians still lead the pack in sheer bravado, but regional styles emerging in other sections of the U.S. and around the Pacific Rim could challenge the dominance of Napa Valley's elite.

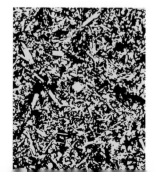

▲ Label for **Louis Martini Winery**. Design Firm: **Ortega Design;** Designers: **Joann Ortega, Susann Ortega;** Hand Lettering: **Joann Ortega**

Louis M. Martini is the oldest family-owned winery in the Napa Valley. For Martini's trio of high-end restaurant wines, the designers set out to create a label that would look contemporary, but have a sense of the classic nature of the vintner's art. The black background of the label blends with the dark wines, but the matte texture of the paper creates a subtle textural difference between it and the sheen of the glass bottle. A redesign of the winery's Napa Valley Reserve Cabernet Sauvignon (top right) features an abstract drawing of the original vignette rendered in soft pastel hues.

❖ Label for **TarraWarra Vineyards**.
Design Firm: **Cato Design Inc.;**
Designers: **Cato Design Inc.**

The language of the Australian
aborigines is full of words that
are sonorous to Western ears.
TarraWarra Vineyards takes its
name from one of these. And
while the name is ancient, the
imagery is certainly not. Clean,
contemporary graphics suggest the energetic qualities of
this Australian Chardonnay.

▲ **Star Hill Chardonnay** label for **Star Hill Winery**. Design Firm: **Colonna, Farrell: Strategic Marketing & Design;** Art Director: **Ralph Colonna;** Designer/Illustrator: **Amy Racina**

The Star Hill label wasn't designed exclusively for retail. The Goldenbergs, owners of Star Hill Winery, sell the vintage primarily at fine California-style restaurants such as Wolfgang Puck's Spago in Los Angeles. The objective was to create a label that would fit in with the upscale, ultra-contemporary feeling of these restaurants yet be distinctive enough for patrons to recognize the label from several tables away.

❖ **Picnic** wine label for **Sunny St. Helena Winery**. Design Firm: **Colonna, Farrell: Strategic Marketing & Design** Art Director: **Ralph Colonna;** Designer: **Susan Handly**

For a small run of a light table wine, St. Helena asked Colonna, Farrell for a label that would project a fun, airy feeling—a wine perfect for picnics.

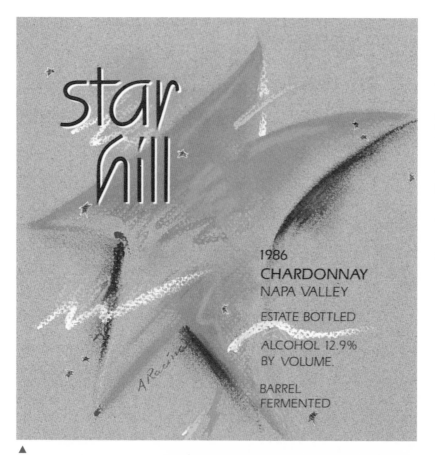

▲

❖

■ **Nouveau** for **Sebastiani Vine-yards**. Design Firm: **Tharp Did It;** Art Director/Designer/Illustrator: **Rick Tharp**

Gamay Beaujolais, or Nouveau, is traditionally the first wine to market from a particular harvest. Sebastiani asked for a label that would reflect the fresh, spontaneous character of this wine, so Rick Tharp borrowed a bit from Alexander Calder and Miro—whose freshness he's always admired—to capture that feeling. The labels were printed in four PMS colors plus varnish on Simpson C1S.

▲ Gift wine for **The Duffy Design Group**. Design Firm: **The Duffy Design Group**; Art Director/Designer/Illustrator: **Sara Ledgard**

Each year around Christmas, The Duffy Design Group sends a limited-edition gift wine to the firm's friends and clients. And each year, the design is done by a different designer. The bottle for the 1988 holidays was created by Sara Ledgard. The graphics were silkscreened directly onto the glass.

❖ Label for **Round Hill Winery**. Design Firm: **Colonna, Farrell: Strategic Marketing & Design** Art Director: **Ralph Colonna**; Designer: **Amy Racina**; Printer: **Herdell Printing**

A premium varietal, Round Hill is sold primarily at retail. This label was intended to provide instant brand recognition and strong shelf presence, as well as make an attractive mass display. The label features an embossed image of the winery's new facility and was printed on 70-pound Beckett Cambric.

▲

❖

KENWOOD

**SONOMA VALLEY
CABERNET
SAUVIGNON
1•9•8•5**

ARTIST SERIES
PRODUCED & BOTTLED BY KENWOOD VINEYARDS
KENWOOD, CALIFORNIA   ALC. 12.5 BY VOLUME

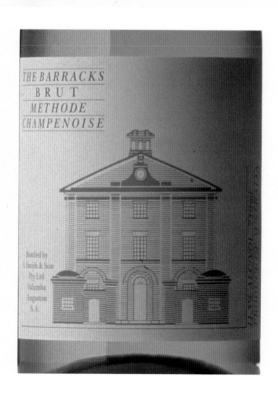

■ Label for **Kenwood Vineyards**. Design Firm: **Image Group, Inc.**; Art Director: **Tom Armstrong**; Designers: **Tom Armstrong, Chris Cornelssen**; Illustrator: **Steve Jensen**

Wine lovers and collectors the world over anxiously await each year's new release in the Kenwood Artist Series Cabernet Sauvignon. The labels feature the work of well-known contemporary artists. The 1985 vintage showcases "Red Letter to Joe," a contemporary, multi-media work. The label was printed in four-color process on white Kromekote with gold foil stamping and a gloss varnish.

● **The Barracks** label for **S. Smith & Son Pty. Ltd**. Design Firm: **Cato Design Inc.**; Designers: **Cato Design Inc.**

This unusual approach to champagne takes its cue from the name of the product: The Barracks. The illustration mimics a blueprint elevation, providing a quick visual identifier.

☆ **Verduzzo** label for **Tesco**. Design Firm: **Michael Peters + Partners**; Art Director/Designer: **Kathy Miller**; Photographer: **Carl Warner**

A photograph—rather than the more usual illustration—of a bunch of grapes set against white Italian marble make a novel and appropriate visual for this dry white Italian wine.

▲ **Sonoma County Red Table Wine** for **California Wine Wizards.** Design Firm: **Colonna, Farrell: Strategic Marketing & Design;** Art Director: **Ralph Colonna;** Designer: **Jill Regan;** Illustrator: **Mike Gray**

Isn't this character precious? And what an unexpected pleasure to come across a label that's decked out in stars and moons against a red, white and blue palette. The label was created for the annual California Wine Wizards Contest. It's printed on Beckett Cambric stock in two match colors.

❖ **1984 Cabernet Sauvignon** for **Inglenook-Napa Valley.** Design Firm: **Colonna, Farrell: Strategic Marketing & Design;** Art Director: **Ralph Colonna;** Designers: **John Farrell, Ralph Colonna**

The classic insignia of this Chardonnay varietal took "Best of Show" at the 1987 California State Fair. The embossed Victoria monogram of winery founder Gustave Niebaum is accented with grape clusters and printed in burgundy, gold and black inks.

■ **20/20 Wine Cooler** for **The Wine Group.** Design Firm: **Axion Design Inc.;** Art Director: **Robert P. deVito;** Designers: **Anne Cook, Lisa Brussell;** Lettering: **Anne Cook;** Illustrator: **Suzanne Holm**

Bright, berry-like colors emphasize the fruit flavors and position this cooler as a "fun" alternative to more serious wines. The well-known 20/20 brand mark was given a new look and placed prominently on the neck band, main label and six-pack carrier.

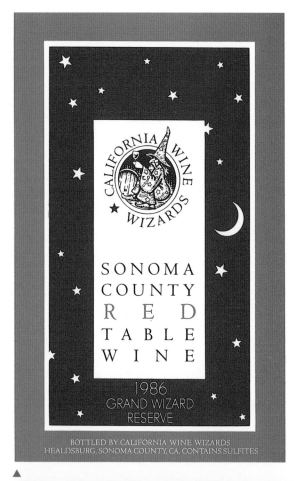

LINDEMANS

MIRRABOOK

1987

Rhine Riesling

When Dr Henry John Lindeman first began making wine
in 1843, his vision was that Australian wines would one day
the very best from anywhere in the world. This tradition of ex.
has produced a succession of truly world class wines, and wines
as this, offering world class value in sought after varietals.
To commemorate this Australian winemaking achievement we have
named the wines Mirrabook, the Aboriginal word
for Southern Cross.

2 LITRES

● **Mirrabook** 2-litre wine cask for **Lindemans Wine Pty. Ltd., Australia**. Design Firm: **Cato Design Inc.;** Designers: **Cato Design Inc.**

What better symbol for world-class Australian wines than the Southern Cross constellation? The name of the wine—Mirrabook—is the Aboriginal name for the constellation. The saturated, earthy colors suggest the Outback at dusk.

▲ **Gustave Niebaum Collection** for **Inglenook-Napa Valley**. Design Firm: **Colonna, Farrell: Strategic Marketing & Design;** Art Director: **John Farrell;** Designers: **John Farrell, Amy Racina;** Illustrator: **John Farrell;** Printer: **FP Label**

Inglenook designates these super-premiums by the vineyard where the grapes were grown. Metallic foil accentuates the image of quality and the illustrations of each of the vineyards.

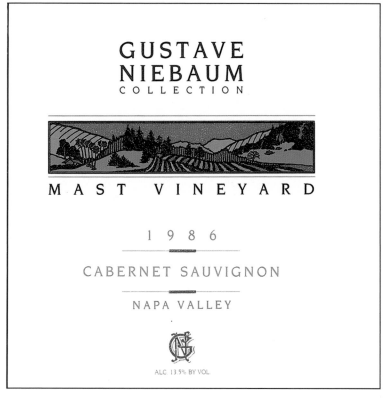

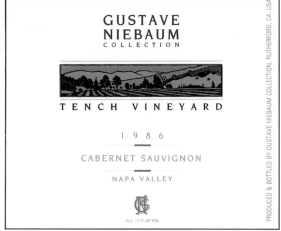

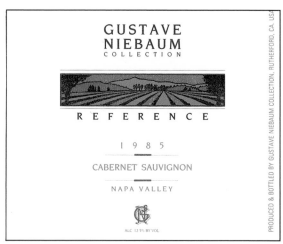

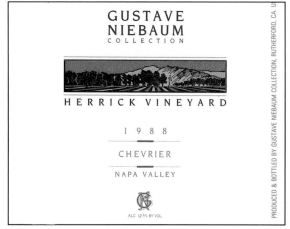

❖ **Montage** label for **Christian Brothers**. Design Firm: **Broom & Broom, Inc.;** Art Director: **David Broom;** Designers: **David Broom, Kimiko Murakami Chan**

The name and image were created for this unique product—a blend of French and American varietal wines. The richly textured paper is 70-pound Beckett Brilliant Opaque vellum with gold foil stamping.

▲ **Mr. MacGregor's Chardonnay** for **Karly Wines**. Design Firm: **Colonna, Farrell: Strategic Marketing & Design;** Art Director: **John Farrell;** Designers: **John Farrell, Chris Mathes;** Illustrator: **Beth Whybrow Leeds**

What else could you put on a label for Mr. MacGregor's wines but a rabbit? The soft colors and watercolor styling are pure Beatrix Potter.

❖ **Monte Rosso** for **Louis Martini Winery**. Design Firm: **Ortega Design;** Designers: **Joann Ortega, Susann Ortega;** Illustrator: **Remington Martini**

The Los Ninos label was created by the Martini family to commemorate the birth of their children. Each year a child is born, a special Cabernet Sauvignon is reserved. When the child is old enough to paint or draw, a label is designed. Ortega Design selected this drawing by Remington Martini, age three. The vintage is sold only at the winery in St. Helena, California.

■ **Lost Hills Cooler** for **Lost Hills Vineyards**. Design Firm: **Tharp Did It;** Art Director/Designer: **Rick Tharp;** Illustrators: **Rick Tharp, Georgia Deaver**

The market is literally awash in wine cooler brands, making entry risky. Lost Hills asked Rick Tharp to adapt the winery logo he had previously designed for use on this cooler.

● **Antares Wine** for **Hacienda Winery**. Design Firm: **Image Group, Inc.;** Art Director/Designer: **Suzanne Bastear**

Antares—a giant red star of the first magnitude—was selected as the name for this new premium Bordeaux style wine. The label had to position the wine in the upper end of the red wine market. The black, gloss-finished background was carefully selected to blend with a full bottle, while the prismatic burst of color suggests a star.

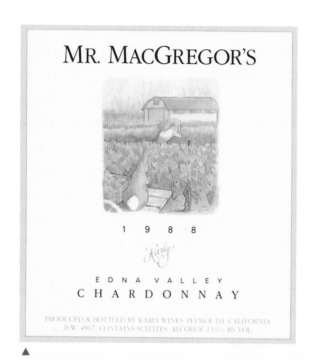

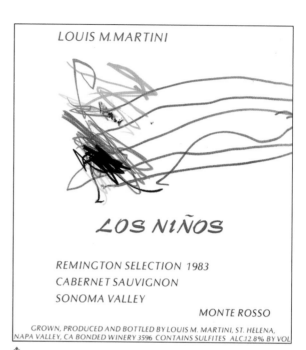

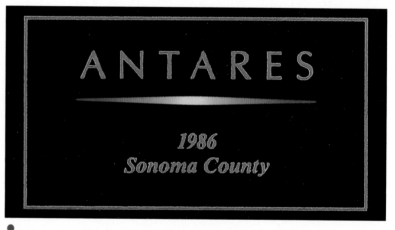

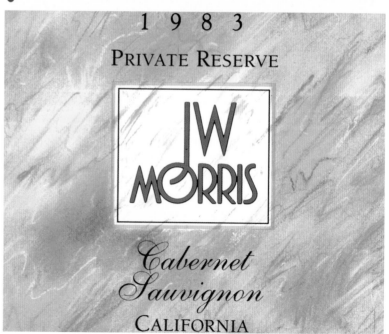

☆ **1983 Cabernet Sauvignon** for **J.W. Morris Winery**. Design Firm: **Colonna, Farrell: Strategic Marketing & Design;** Art Director: **Ralph Colonna;** Designer: **Cynthia Maguire;** Illustrator: **Beth Whybrow Leeds**

A contemporary, yet restrained, background gives J.W. Morris wine an air of quiet sophistication. The logo provides quick brand recognition at retail and the colors make a memorable impression when massed on a store shelf.

🍇 **Olivet Lane** label for **Pellegrini Family Vineyards**. Design Firm: **Colonna, Farrell: Strategic Marketing & Design;** Art Director: **Ralph Colonna;** Designer: **Cynthia Maguire;** Illustrator: **Beth Whybrow Leeds**

A soft, pictorial landscape, a "family crest" and an Italianate border combine to give this choice chardonnay a proper estate-bottled image.

▲ **Rebling Pfirsich Cooler** for **Seagram GmbH.** Design Firm: **Knut Hartmann Design;** Art Director/Designer: **Knut Hartmann;** Illustrator: **Klaus Albrecht**

Hip graphics for a hip product—a wine cooler marketed in West Germany. Printed four color offset.

❖ **Delicato "Minis"** for **Delicato Winery.** Design Firm: **Colonna, Farrell: Strategic Marketing & Design;** Art Director: **Ralph Colonna;** Designer: **Peggy Koch**

Soft colors and a finely-detailed illustration of the vineyards create a look that's as delicate as the product itself.

■ **1987** and **1988 Sauvignon Blanc labels** for **Robert Pecota Winery.** Designer: **Robert Pecota;** Illustrators: **Mortimer Kohn** (1987), **Phoebe Ellsworth** (1988)

Since 1973, the Robert Pecota Winery has featured the paintings of local artists on the labels of its Sauvignon Blanc and Cabernet Sauvignon wines. Consumers now tend to identify the vintage by the illustration. Mortimer Kohn's work is entitled "In Her Mind;" Phoebe Ellsworth's piece is called "Sunflowers." Both labels are printed four color.

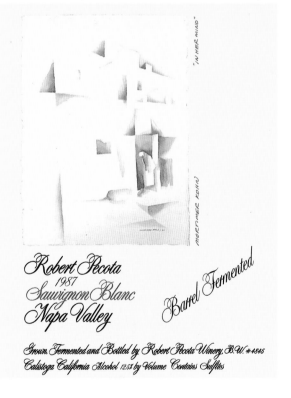

▲ **Kenwood Cabernet Sauvignon Artist Series** for **Kenwood Vineyards.** Design Firm: **Image Group, Inc.;** Art Director: **Tom Armstrong;** Designers: **Tom Armstrong, Chris Cornelssen;** Illustrator: **Alan Wolton**

The wine for the Artist Series is personally chosen by winemaker Michael Lee, who looks for barrels of Cabernet Sauvignon that show exceptional promise and character. The 1984 label features a richly-textured, Impressionistic oil painting by Alan Wolton depicting Montana de Oro State Park in California. Printed in four colors with silver foil and gloss varnish on Kromekote white stock.

❖ **Cabernet Sauvignon** for **Domaine Michel.** Design Firm: **Ortega Design;** Designers: **Joann Ortega, Susann Ortega**

Winery owner Jacque Michel of Switzerland wanted to capture the status of California wines and European tradition in the label design for his new wines. The embossed "shadow" letterform of the winery name is prominent against a subtle linen textured paper. Colors associated with California and the Mediterranean were speced for the horizontal bands.

■ **Silver Lake Cabernet Sauvignon** for **Washington Wine & Beverage.** Design Firm: **Tim Girvin Design, Inc.;** Art Director: **Tim Girvin;** Designer: **Laurie Vette**

Silver Lake is a moderately-priced brand that needed to be marketed in all the usual ways. Combining a variety of techniques—embossing, silver foil stamping and a subtle design—Tim Girvin Design was able to achieve an memorable look with a limited budget.

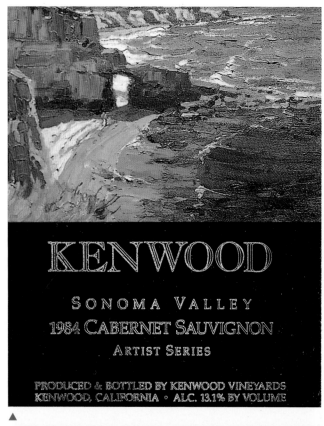

▲

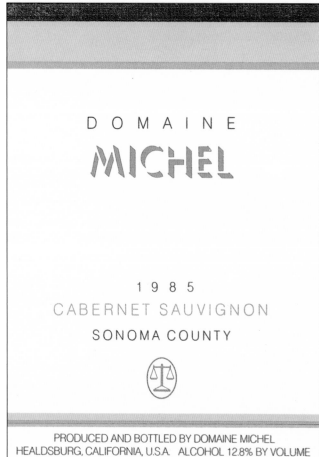

❖

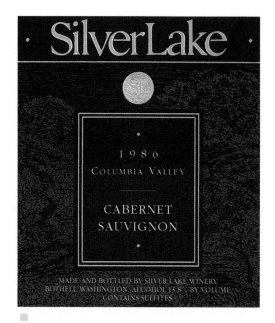

■

●

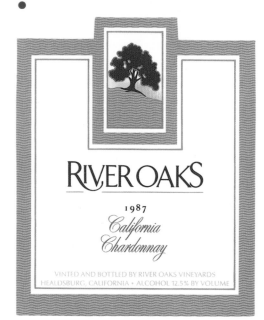

☆

● **Private label** for **Westin Hotels & Resorts, Chateau Ste. Michelle.** Design Firm: **Tim Girvin Design, Inc.;** Art Director/Designer/Illustrator: **Tim Girvin;** Production: **Peg Ogle**

Westin Hotels and Resorts are internationally recognized as premier executive-class establishments. Tim Girvin Design was asked to create a private label for the wines, which are served in the chain's restaurants, that would blend with the typically elegant dining areas and portray the modern and sophisticated image the chain desired.

☆ **1987 California Chardonnay** for **River Oaks Vineyards.** Design Firm: **Colonna, Farrell: Strategic Marketing & Design;** Art Directors: **Ralph Colonna, Carol Dennison;** Designer: **Joann Street;** Illustrator: **Carol Dennison**

A subtle background pattern resembling waves and a strong typographic treatment combine to give this label a "double reading." From a distance, the strong verticals and large type provide quick brand recognition; up close the pastel colors behind the oak tree emblem and thin metallic gold elements create a rich, textured feeling. Printed in five PMS colors on Coronado Opaque stock.

🍷 **1989 Nouveau** for **Sebastiani Vineyards.** Design Firm: **Tharp Did It;** Art Director/Designer/Illustrator: **Rick Tharp**

Gamay Beaujolais—the first wine bottled from a harvest—is rich, fresh and fruity. Sebastiani changes its Nouveau graphics each year (another Nouveau label is featured on page 115), searching for a look that will say young, exuberant and maybe a bit daring.

▲ **Franzia White Zinfandel Wine Cooler** for **The Wine Group.** Design Firm: **Axion Design Inc.;** Art Director: **Robert P. deVito;** Designer: **Lisa Brussell**

Playing on the subtle blush color of the beverage, Axion puts the buyer's focus on a circular brand mark featuring an illustration of grapes rendered in soft colors. Extending the letter "R" in a sweeping curve and setting the brand name in gold foil stamping lends a classic, elegant look to the design.

❖ White and Red wines for **the Royal Hotel.** Design Firm: **Cato Design Inc.;** Designers: **Cato Design Inc.**

For the Royal Hotel in Sydney, Australia, Cato Design "ripped off" the traditional wine label—literally. The fragmentary image in the upper left hand corner communicates the standard messages: quality, taste, tradition.

■ **Private Reserve Napa Valley Chardonnay** for **Forest Hill Vineyard.** Design Firm: **Primo Angeli Inc.;** Creative Director: **Primo Angeli;** Designer: **Ray Honda**

Forest Hill is a small Napa Valley winery that produces a limited amount of high-quality chardonnay. The client wanted a design that would capture the essence of their quality wine with as few graphics and words as possible. A clear bottle—rarely used for chardonnays—showcases the product, while the graphics hint at the rolling hills and fog of the Napa Valley.

▲ Label for **Troquato Vineyards**. Design Firm: **Tharp Did It**; Art Director: **Rick Tharp**; Designers: **Rick Tharp, Karen "Kimi" Nomura**; Illustrator: **Karen "Kimi" Nomura**; Printer: **Blake Printery**

For its Johannisberg Riesling, Troquato Vineyards wanted to include a rendering of the two stone mountain lions which guard the entrance to the town of Los Gatos ("The Cats"). The same type treatment and logo were carried over to the Zinfandel label, where a medallion commemorating the town's centennial was added.

❖ Labels for **Jepson Vineyards**. Design Firm: **Akagi Design**; Art Director/Designer: **Doug Akagi**

These two labels for Richard Leland of Jepson Vineyards represent the extremes for label designers. The Chardonnay (left) had a label; designer Doug Akagi simply updated and refined it. For the brandy (right), however, Akagi used multiple typefaces to recreate the look of an 18th century French brandy label. Alambic pot distilling—the method used to make the Jepson brandy —came into wide use in France during that time.

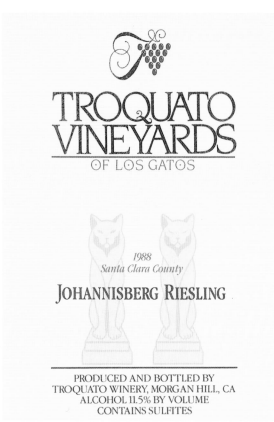

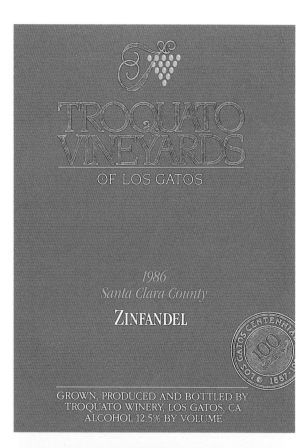

Franzia Cabernet Sauvignon label for **The Wine Group**. Design Firm: **Axion Design Inc.;** Art Director: **Robert P. deVito;** Designer: **Lisa Brussell**

A classic-style illustration of grapes puts the focus of this label squarely on the product. The large logotype provides quick brand recognition and the UPC code on the front of the label makes for quick scanning at mass-market outlets.

▲ **Cabernet Sauvignon** label for **Beechwood Cellars.** Design Firm: **The Graphics Studio;** Art Director/Designer: **Gerry Rosentswieg**

Beechwood Cellars, a boutique winery in Los Angeles, California, wanted a label that was inexpensive, conservative and distinctive. The die-cut edges set this label apart from others on a retail shelf.

❖ House wine for **Cocolezzone.** Design Firm: **The Duffy Design Group;** Art Director/Designer/ Illustrator: **Haley Johnson**

Cocolezzone is an Italian restaurant with casual old-world flair. The wine bottle contains the eatery's house wine, which can be purchased as a gift or used in the restaurant. Designer Haley Johnson updates the familiar checkerboard pattern associated with Italian restaurants, and sets it against black etched glass. Silkscreened in six colors.

▲   ❖

■ Self-promotional wine. Design Firm: **Walcott-Ayers & Shore;** Art Director: **Jim Walcott-Ayers;** Designers: **Stephanie Zurek, Jordana Welles;** Illustrator: **Stephanie Zurek;** Copywriter: **Jim Walcott-Ayers**

Walcott-Ayers & Shore gave this self-promotional champagne to its clients during the Christmas holidays. Aside from the obvious holiday connection, the name "Rudolph's Leap" is also a pun appreciated by the studio's winery clients. Fluorescent magenta and yellow were substituted in the four-color process, and metallic inks were used for the copy and the snowflakes, all contributing to a festive holiday look.

▲ **Jory Champagne** for **Jory Winery.** Design Firm: **Tharp Did It;** Art Director: **Rick Tharp;** Designers: **Kim Tomlinson, Rick Tharp**

The designers wanted to break with tradition by relocating mandatory label information to the neck label, thereby allowing for a more playful use of design elements on the front label. The logotype was placed on the back of the neck band so it wouldn't interfere with the overall graphic theme.

▲

❖ **Big Sur** wines for **Monterey Peninsula Winery.** Design Firm: **Tharp Did It;** Art Director/Designer: **Rick Tharp;** Photographer: **Batista Moon;** Printer: **Blake Printery**

This is a redesign of a label for an inexpensive wine aimed at the tourist trade. The designers took a "postcard" approach by using photography. A "cool" sunrise was shot for the white wine, a "warm" sunset for the red varietal. Four colors and one PMS color were printed on Astolux stock with a varnish.

▲ Wine labels for **Lindemans Wine Pty. Ltd., Australia.** Design Firm: **Cato Design Inc.;** Designers: **Cato Design Inc.**

The international reputation of Australian wines is growing rapidly—as are the variety and sophistication of Australian wine labels. Much more likely to follow in the tradition of California than of Europe, the labels —such as these for Lindemans Chardonnay and Pinot Noir wines—seem to combine classic charm with a twist of the contemporary in just the right proportions.

❖ **Champagne** label for **Coventry Vale Vintners**. Design Firm: **Tim Girvin Design, Inc.;** Art Director/Designer: **Tim Girvin**

Exuberant graphics portray Coventry Vale's mid-price champagne as a fun, quality product—perhaps something to be bought for a birthday or a weekend party—as opposed to the heavy, classic look of more expensive, special-occasion champagnes.

LACEY LᴬMASTER NELSON FARMER INC.

MERLOT

1986

VINTAGE RED WINE

ROUND HILL VINEYARDS
ST. HELENA, CALIFORNIA

ALCOHOL 12.9% BY VOLUME. CONTAINS SULFITES

▪ Wine labels for **Belvedere Winery**. Design Firm: **Colonna, Farrell: Strategic Marketing & Design;** Art Director: **Ralph Colonna;** Designer: **Amy Racina**

Belvedere's range of vineyard-designated wines were brought into a unified graphic system that says premium quality and projects a strong brand image. The labels are printed on 70-pound Kromekote with a gloss varnish and gold foiling.

● Gift wine label for **Lacey LaMaster Nelson Farmer Inc**. Design Firm: **Designed Marketing;** Art Director/Designer: **Bob Upton;** Producer: **Carol Johnson**

As a Christmas gift for its clients, Lacey LaMaster Nelson Farmer Inc. commissioned a lively label for red wine made by Round Hill Vineyards.

BELVEDERE™

YORK CREEK

VINEYARDS

1984 NAPA VALLEY
CABERNET SAUVIGNON

PRODUCED AND BOTTLED BY BELVEDERE WINERY, HEALDSBURG, SONOMA COUNTY, CA. ALCOHOL 13.3% BY VOL. CONTAINS SULFITES

▲ **Amorosa Semi-dry Blush Wine** for **Las Viñas Winery.** Design Firm: **Colonna, Farrell: Strategic Marketing & Design;** Art Director: **Ralph Colonna;** Designer: **Tony Auston**

This is the only entry in the wine category to have used a graduated color background. The label for a companion varietal, Symphony, was printed in a pale green tone. Both are accented with gold foil stamping.

❖ **California "Rosetta"** for **Glen Oaks Cellars.** Design Firm: **Ortega Design;** Designers: **Joann Ortega, Susann Ortega**

Glen Oaks was originally produced and positioned for the Japanese market in three varieties: Classic White, Rosetta and Chianti. The label uses a subtle Italian palette and a gray window effect to give it a gentle, evening atmosphere, reminiscent of a glen at sunset.

■ **Red and White** wines for **Kinselas.** Design Firm: **Cato Design Inc.;** Designers: **Cato Design Inc.**

Kinselas is a famous cabaret restaurant in Sydney, Australia's Oxford Square. Cato Design took a straightforward approach in designing the label for the restaurant's house wine, allowing the brilliant color of the vintages to take center stage.

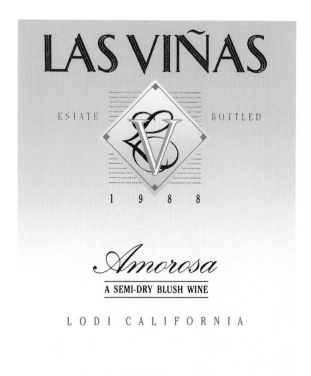

● **Napa Ridge** wine for **Beringer Vineyards.** Design Firm: **Broom & Broom, Inc.;** Art Director: **David Broom;** Designers: **David Broom, Kimiko Murakami Chan;** Calligrapher: **Sandra Bruce**

Napa Ridge is a California wine sold in hotels and restaurants. To achieve an upscale look, Broom & Broom printed a classic sans serif typeface in gold foil accented by gentle brush strokes—one in a blue/gray hue. The labels were printed on 60-pound Estate #4 and finished in machine varnish, straight cut.

▲ **Chandler's Crabhouse** wine for **Schwartz Brothers Restaurants**. Design Firm: **Tim Girvin Design, Inc.;** Art Director: **Tim Girvin;** Designer: **Laurie Vette;** Illustrator: **Tim Girvin**

This private label Chardonnay for a seafood restaurant in Washington state displays an appropriately salty illustration.

❖ **Magnolia Ridge** wine for **Charles Shaw Winery**. Design Firm: **Colonna, Farrell: Strategic Marketing & Design** Art Director: **Ralph Colonna;** Designer: **Susan Handly**

The freshness of just-bottled Gamay Beaujolais is captured in the freshness of a magnolia bud. The subtle coloring contributes to the impression of quality and makes an attractive mass display at retail.

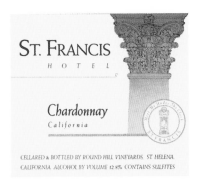

Private label for the **St. Francis Hotel**. Design Firm: **Rene Yung Communications Design Inc.;** Art Director/Designer: **Rene Yung;** Illustrators: **Judith Tan, Rene Yung**

Calling the St. Francis a hotel is like calling Buckingham Palace a townhouse: It is a legendary San Francisco establishment. In creating an identity for the hostelry's house brands, Rene Yung was asked to project a contemporary image while preserving and reflecting the hotel's elegance and heritage.

▲ **1987 Gamay Beaujolais Blanc** for **Sunny St. Helena Winery;** Design Firm: **Colonna, Farrell: Strategic Marketing & Design;** Art Director: **Ralph Colonna;** Designer: **Susan Handly;** Illustrator: **Earl Thollander**

Back when wineries were owned and run by sole proprietors and families, it was popular to make an illustration of the building or surrounding land the focus of the label. As more wine brands are being produced by companies which own neither vineyards or wineries, this technique has been abandoned. Thankfully, there are outfits like the Sunny St. Helena Winery that can still boast of its home-grown vintages through a charming illustration. Printed in four colors plus one PMS color on Beckett Cambric Antique stock.

❖ **1985 Chardonnay** for **Hunter Ashby.** Design Firm: **Colonna, Farrell: Strategic Marketing & Design;** Art Director/Designer: **Ralph Colonna**

A hunter's horn, musical notes in the form of colorful squares, and horizontal lines to depict a musical score are all part of this clever design for Hunter Ashby, a Rutherford, California winery. Printed in four colors plus PMS bronze on Simpson C1S.

■ Christmas gift boxes for **Beringer Vineyards.** Design Firm: **Broom & Broom, Inc.;** Art Director: **David Broom;** Designers: **David Broom, Michele Wetherbee;** Illustrator: **David McCall Johnston**

Every year, Beringer Vineyards, a California winery, creates a series of holiday gift boxes with a unique theme. The theme for 1986 was historical, carried out on a six-sided box. Printed in six colors, embossed, with UV varnish.

SUNNY ST. HELENA WINERY

1987

Napa Valley

GAMAY BEAUJOLAIS
BLANC

PRODUCED AND BOTTLED BY SUNNY ST. HELENA WINERY
ST. HELENA, CALIF. USA. CONTAINS SULFITES
ALCOHOL 11.0% BY VOLUME

HUNTER ASHBY

1985 NAPA VALLEY
CHARDONNAY

PRODUCED AND BOTTLED BY HUNTER ASHBY
RUTHERFORD, CALIFORNIA • ALCOHOL 13% BY VOLUME

Self-promotional wine label. Design Firm: **Axion Design Inc.;** Art Director: **James McElheron;** Designer: **Eric Read**

The great thing about creating your own wine label is that there are no rules. Axion took the opportunity to express its style via a collage of geometric shapes, hand-rendered type and bold colors.

▲ **Trois Cordon Collection** labels for **Trois Cordon.** Design Firm: **Ortega Design;** Designers/Illustrators: **Susann Ortega, Joann Ortega**

Featured are two designs from a series of labels created for Les Vines Skalli, a French winery. The winery admired the success of California wine and the style of its labels, and wanted a look that would be attractive to young consumers in France. Designers Susann and Joann Ortega adapted a graphic composition of vineyards found in the south of France. Fresh pastel colors speak of the gentle aromatic bouquet found in these soft- and medium-body wines.

❖ Varietal labels for **Rutherford Estates.** Design Firm: **Colonna, Farrell: Strategic Marketing & Design;** Art Director: **John Farrell;** Designer: **Cynthia Maguire**

A unique use of splash graphics, this label design for Rutherford Estates uses bright yellow and strong burgundy hues against a subtle gray grid. A mixture of typefaces are printed in black, gold foil and warm gray. Printed in three colors and gold foil stamping on Beckett Cambric stock.

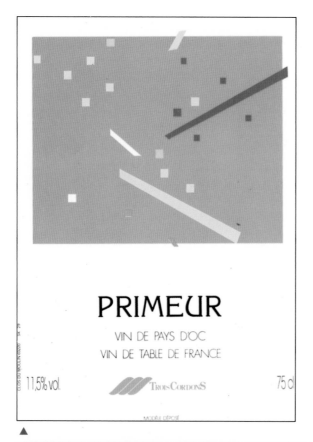

Proprietor's Reserve packaging for Glen Ellen Winery. Design Firm: Colonna, Farrell: Strategic Marketing & Design; Art Director/Designer/Illustrator: John Farrell

To create a refreshing, home-spun image for this Sonoma County, California winery, Colonna, Farrell designed a highly-visual logo, fitting it into a unique curved window shape and then refining the graphics to illustrate the warmth and richness of the winery experience. The result: a "user-friendly" label that has helped make this family winery popular with customers and growers. Printed in four colors plus one PMS color and gold foil embossed on Simpson Estate stock.

▲ **Tin Pony** label for **Iron Horse Vineyards**. Design Firm: **Colonna, Farrell: Strategic Marketing & Design** Art Director: **Ralph Colonna;** Designer/Illustrator: **Joann Ortega**

A whimsical parade of carousel horses floats across the label for this generic table wine. The Tin Pony name is an appropriate name for the the "younger brother" of the winery's premium brand, Iron Horse.

❖ Label for **Thomas Jaeger Winery**. Design Firm: **The Weller Institute for the Cure of Design, Inc.;** Art Director/Designer: **Don Young;** Illustrator: **Don Weller**

A portrait of Bacchus, the Greek god of wine, was rendered as a bunch of grapes for this unusual specialty wine.

■ **Mosaic** label for **deLorimer Winery**. Design Firm: **Colonna, Farrell: Strategic Marketing & Design;** Art Director: **Ralph Colonna;** Designers: **Joann Street, Ralph Colonna**

For this expensive blended wine, Colonna, Farrell chose deep, saturated hues, a traditional color palette and gold foil to create an image that says "expensive—and worth it."

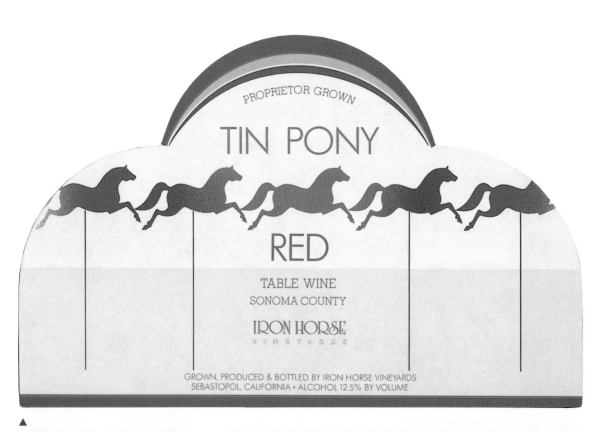

PROPRIETOR GROWN

TIN PONY

RED

TABLE WINE
SONOMA COUNTY

IRON HORSE
VINEYARDS

GROWN, PRODUCED & BOTTLED BY IRON HORSE VINEYARDS
SEBASTOPOL, CALIFORNIA • ALCOHOL 12.5% BY VOLUME

▲

❖

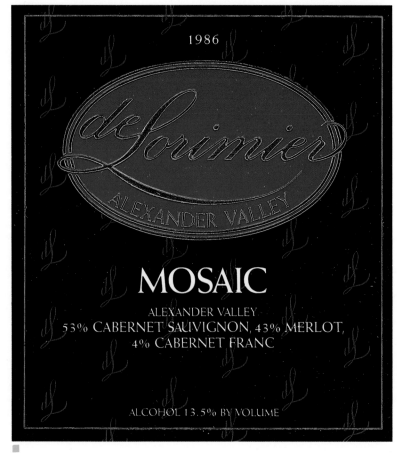

1986

deLorimier
ALEXANDER VALLEY

MOSAIC

ALEXANDER VALLEY
53% CABERNET SAUVIGNON, 43% MERLOT,
4% CABERNET FRANC

ALCOHOL 13.5% BY VOLUME

■

R E S E R V E

Donn Chappellet

1985
Napa Valley
Cabernet Sauvignon

PRODUCED
AND BOTTLED
BY CHAPPELLET
VINEYARD
PRITCHARD HILL
ST. HELENA
CA. U.S.A.
B.W. 4537
ALC. 12.8% BY VOL.
CONTAINS SULFITES

CHAPPELLET

1987
Napa Valley
Johannisberg Riesling

PRODUCED
AND BOTTLED
BY CHAPPELLET
VINEYARD
PRITCHARD HILL
ST. HELENA
CA. U.S.A.
B.W. 4537
ALC. 11.1% BY VOL
CONTAINS SULFITES
RES. SUGAR 1.3% BY VOL

● Labels for **Chappellet Vine-yard**. Design Firm: **Colonna, Farrell: Strategic Marketing & Design;** Art Director: **Ralph Colonna;** Designer: **Joann Street**

The subtlety of white and the drama of brilliant red are complemented by an embossed symbol and logo for this expensive varietal wine.

☆ **Frederico Benegas** wine label for **Le Vignoble**. Designer: **Eduardo A. Cànovas**

A new label was developed as part of an overall identity program for Frederico Benegas cellars, a hundred-year-old Argentine vintner.

▲ **Gloria Ferrer** wine label for **Freixenet Sonoma Champagne.** Design Firm: **Colonna, Farrell: Strategic Marketing & Design;** Art Director: **John Farrell;** Designers: **Michelle Collier, Ralph Colonna, John Farrell**

Gloria Ferrer, a subsidiary of Freixenet in Spain, had a marketing problem: a quality champagne that was experiencing slow sales due to a low-price image. A new logo was developed to give focus and identity to the name. Also, the logo/leaf concept was expanded and adapted to work on all parts of the new package. The front label piece was contoured to recall the outline of the Spanish buildings used in the champagne's production.

❖ **Merlot** label for **Bidwell Vineyards.** Design Firm: **Ortega Design;** Designers: **Joann Ortega, Susann Ortega;** Illustrator: **Susann Ortega**

The contemporary subtlety of the colors and forms of this label accent the striking prominence of the winery's classic name. The type forms and illustration convey the long heritage of New York's Long Island region.

■ **Cabernet Sauvignon** label for **Wilhelmina Vineyards.** Design Firm: **Colonna, Farrell: Strategic Marketing & Design;** Art Director: **Ralph Colonna;** Designer/Illustrator: **Joann Ortega**

The owners of this small winery located on a hillside in California's Napa Valley wanted to capture their Dutch heritage without using traditional symbols—windmills, wooden shoes, tulips—in the usual way. This illustration of a tulip is rendered "California-style." Printed in four colors with two PMS colors and embossed in gold foil on Coronado Opaque stock.

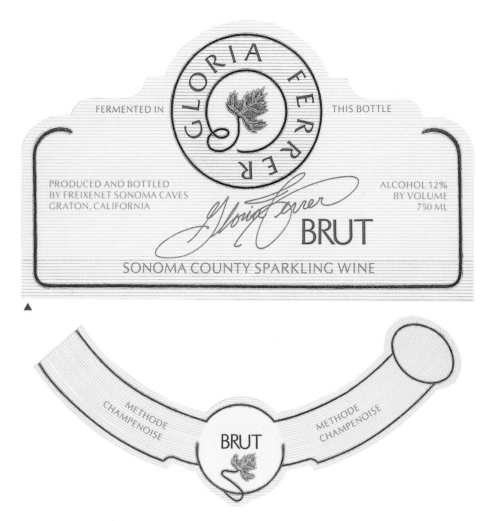

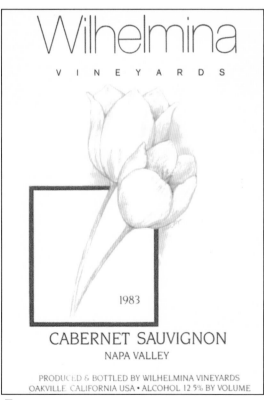

● Labels for **Zaca Mesa Winery.**
Design Firm: **The Graphics Studio;** Art Director/Designer/Illustrator: **Gerry Rosentswieg**

These are promotional labels produced for the Los Angeles Philharmonic. Labels featured in the top photo and the close-up were created to celebrate the 25th Anniversary of the orchestra. An abstract "25" played off the successful label design of the previous year (bottom left), which featured an abstract rendering of a treble clef.

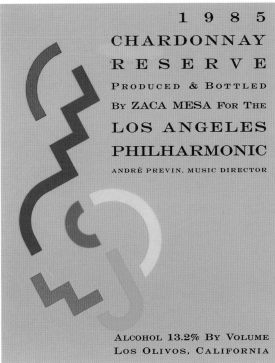

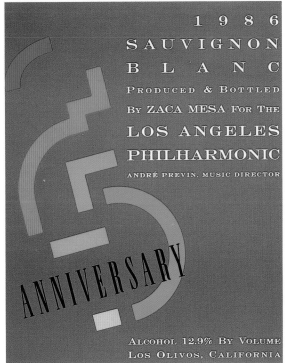

▲ **La Marjolaine** wine labels for **Domaine Michel**. Design Firm: **Ortega Design**; Designers: **Joann Ortega, Susann Ortega**

Named for the Swiss estate of Jean-Jacque Michel, European vintner and owner of Domaine Michel, La Marjolaine features the balance scale logo previously developed by Ortega Design for the Domaine Michel label (see page 126).

❖ Packaging and label for **Randstad Uitzendbureau**. Design Firm: **Total Design, b.v.;** Designer: **Sacha Joseph**

This private label developed for the Randstad employment agency uses a map and large type to celebrate the Bergerac region of France, where the wine was made.

LA MARJOLAINE

1 9 8 3

CABERNET SAUVIGNON
SONOMA COUNTY

CELLARED AND BOTTLED BY LA MARJOLAINE
HEALDSBURG, CALIFORNIA U.S.A. ALCOHOL 13 % BY VOLUME

LA MARJOLAINE

CHARDONNAY
SONOMA COUNTY
1 9 8 4

CELLARED AND BOTTLED BY LA MARJOLAINE
HEALDSBURG, CALIFORNIA U.S.A. ALCOHOL 12.5% BY VOLUME

Pastel wine label for **Mirassou Vineyards**. Design Firm: **Tharp And/Or Marchionna**; Art Directors/Designers: **Rick Tharp, Thom Marchionna**; Illustrator: **James Lamarche**; Hand lettering: **Rick Tharp, Tim Girvin**; Printer: **Blake Printery**

The designers wanted a soft, pastoral feel to complement the delicate color of this blush wine targeted to women. Simpson Sundance Felt paper was selected to enhance the reproduction of the painting, which was originally done on watercolor paper.

▲ **Eye of the Swan** & **Black Beauty** wines for **Sebastiani Vineyards.** Design Firm: **Tharp Did It;** Art Director: **Rick Tharp;** Designers: **Rick Tharp, Karen "Kimi" Nomura;** Illustrator: **Michael Bull;** Printer: **Blake Printery**

The label was designed to complement the color of the wine, which is the same copper color as the iris of the Australian Black Swan. The designers integrated the UPC code into the delicate design by transforming it into a "field" of cattails. Printed in three PMS colors and one Toyo color on Simpson C1S stock. A tinted varnish adds a protective coating.

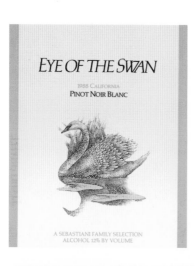

EYE OF THE SWAN

Eye of the Swan, taking its name from the copper-colored iris of the Australian Black Swan, is a wine that's unique to Sebastiani. It was first made in 1975 by August Sebastiani, who, besides being a second-generation winemaker, was an avid conservationist and breeder of rare birds.

Made from the noble Pinot Noir grape, the wine's coppery color is created by quickly separating the clear juice of the grapes from the fruit's black skins.

The result is a Pinot Noir Blanc that's delicately dry with an ideal balance of fruit and crispness. Its medium body and lingering finish make it an excellent companion to grilled poultry or veal.

❖ House wines for **The Last Aussie Fishcaf.** Design Firm: **Andrew Bell Graphic Designers;** Designer: **Andrew Bell;** Illustrator: **Ian McCausland**

The labels for these house wines have as much personality as the eatery itself. Playing off the restaurant's name, Andrew Bell incorporated a stylized graphic of a fish into the design, and selected a thin-stroke sans serif type—reversed out in white—to identify each variety.

■ **R Chardonnay** label for the **Rotary Club of St. Helena, California.** Design Firm: **Ortega Design;** Designers: **Joann Ortega, Susann Ortega;** Illustrator: **Joann Ortega**

Wine is such a mainstay of the California wine growing regions that even the Rotary Club has its own brand. The design seeks to project the Rotary's goals to support both local and worldwide understanding, goodwill and peace through international fellowship of men and women. An illustration of the globe conveys the organization's international scope and provides a colorful background to the letter "R," the name of the wine and a phonetic play on the concept of "our" Chardonnay.

1 9 8 7

CHARDONNAY

NAPA VALLEY

VINTED AND BOTTLED BY "R" CELLARS
CALISTOGA CALIFORNIA
ALC. 12.5% BY VOL.

CHARDONNAY
NAPA VALLEY

The objective of the St. Helena Rotary is to encourage and foster service above self. It is in this spirit that we created an extended family with the "R" wine project. With the revenue from this project you, as part of this family will be helping to support both local and world wide understanding, goodwill and peace through international fellowship of men and women united in the ideal of service.

Be a part of the efforts that have helped so many.

CONTAINS SULFITES

LABEL BY ORTEGA DESIGN

▲ Wine label and gift box for **Carneros Quality Alliance**. Design Firm: **Walcott-Ayers & Shore;** Art Director: **Jim Walcott-Ayers;** Designer: **Elisa McWhinney**

The Carneros Quality Alliance is a group of wineries and growers formed to promote the Carneros region of California's Napa and Sonoma valleys. This Carneros Pinot Noir was a blend of lots submitted by the members and was the first "appellation" wine released in the United States. The label bears a stylized ram's head—the group's logo—while the six-bottle box features a map of the region. The map was made around the turn of the century and serves to show literally where Carneros is on the map and to emphasize the heritage of the region as a wine-growing area.

❖ **Country Garden Coolers** for **Barraclough's Soft Drinks**. Design Firm: **Elmwood Design Ltd.;** Designer: **Clare Walker;** Illustrator: **Gill Marklew**

The client, which also makes a variety of soft drinks, asked for an energetic, refreshing look for its line of wine coolers.

1980 NAPA VALLEY **MERLOT**

JAEGER
INGLEWOOD VINEYARD

PRODUCED AND BOTTLED BY JAEGER CELLAR
RUTHERFORD, NAPA VALLEY, CA USA.
ALCOHOL 13.5% BY VOLUME

■ Label for **Louis Martini Winery**.
Design Firm: **Ortega Design**;
Designers: **Joann Ortega, Susann Ortega**

Updating a well-known label is
always a tricky proposition. To
give the Martini labels a more
contemporary look, Ortega Design created a new logotype,
brightened the illustration and
changed the dimensions to
make the label more horizontal.

● **Jaeger** label for **Jaeger Cellar**.
Design Firm: **Colonna, Farrell:
Strategic Marketing & Design**;
Art Directors: **Bill Jaeger III,
Ralph Colonna**; Designer/Illustrator: **Ralph Colonna**

Although the Jaeger family produces only one wine, it is a merlot —a super-premium varietal
which is difficult to make and
even more difficult to make well.
The label emphasizes the name
and contains an image of grapes
to help buyers make the connection between the unusual
variety, the skill of the vintner
and the quality of the wine.

▲ **1987 Pinot Noir** and **1988 Chardonnay** for **Zaca Mesa Winery.** Design Firm: **Colonna, Farrell: Strategic Marketing & Design;** Art Director: **Ralph Colonna;** Designer: **Amy Racina;** Illustrator: **Sebastian Titus**

Over the years, Colonna, Farrell has designed several labels for this large California winery located near Santa Barbara. For this effort, Zaca Mesa was looking for a closer tie-in to the mainline labels while maintaining the distinguished, premium look achieved by designer Wesley Poole, who created the "American Reserve" line labels. Printed in four colors plus one PMS color and gold foil stamping on Simpson C1S paper.

❖ **Chardonnay** and **Pinot Noir** labels for **Bouchaine Vineyards.** Design Firm: **Walcott-Ayers & Shore;** Art Director: **Jim Walcott-Ayers;** Designers: **Jim Walcott-Ayers, Stephanie Zurek, Elisa McWhinney**

When Walcott-Ayers & Shore was commissioned to redesign the Bouchaine labels, it was given two primary objectives. The first was to produce a label that would be simple to duplicate every year without altering the original shape. The Napa, California winery also wanted the label to easily differentiate the red from the white varieties, and to distinguish the regular wines from the reserve bottlings.

PICCOLO

1985 Napa Valley

MERLOT

A Table Wine Vinted and Bottled by

The House of Piccolo

St. Helena, Napa Valley, California

Piccolo table wine label for **House of Piccolo.** Design Firm: **Frazier Design;** Art Director/Designer/Illustrator: **Craig Frazier**

Frazier Design took a whimsical approach with this label design to depict the fantasy of enjoying wine. The graphics are bright and light—everything a good wine should be. Printed in four colors with a varnish.

BEER & LIQUOR

The flurry of excitement created in the mid-1980s by the explosive growth of wine coolers and fruit liqueurs has dispersed. The labeling of distilled spirits has settled back into a comfortable and classicist mode, but there are exciting developments afoot in the beer cooler.

Micro-breweries are the rage of the day. And while there is no industry-wide definition of how few cases a brewery should produce to be called "micro," the public's thirst for brews that promise something more distinctive than the homogenized taste offered by the mega-brand beers seems unquenchable.

Ironically, especially in America, beer drinkers looking for a new twist have not turned to the many fine European small-batch brews such as St. Sixtus. Nor has shandy become popular. Instead, the image of the beer—as projected by its name and packaging—and some special regional association seem to be the key selling points. Pete's Wicked Ale, Cockatoo Lager and Hunde, all featured in this chapter, are prime examples.

Of course, this is terrific news for designers. It both increases the pool of clients and makes the marketers more amenable to solutions that might once have been labeled as "not mainstream enough to battle Budweiser." ◆

New beers are busting out all over, and designers have been quick to move away from the brewing industry's hoary traditions and forge new territory in the quest for brand acceptance.

▲ **The Gleneagles Scotch Whisky** for **Bells.** Design Firm: **Michael Peters + Partners;** Art Director/ Designer: **Glenn Tutssel;** Illustrator: **Roy Knipe**

Avid golfers are familiar with the famous Gleneagle Hotel, a mecca for golf enthusiasts. This private label design capitalizes on the hotel's golfing heritage and tranquil setting.

❖ **Boston Schnapps** for **Glenmore Distillers.** Design Firm: **Mittleman/Robinson Design Associates;** Designer: **Fred Mittleman;** Illustrator: **John Styga**

Schnapps are still popular among consumers ages 21-35. Mittleman/Robinson Design Associates was commissioned to redesign the entire package for the line, including the glass bottle and logo. Using color to identify different flavors is not new; but specing the bands in two tones is unique.

■ **White Rum** for **Fine Fare.** Design Firm: **Michael Peters + Partners;** Art Director/Designer: **Roger Ackroyd**

Sipping on a tall rum and Coke or some other libation made with the tropical liquor conjures up visions of sandy beaches and frothy surf. Designer Roger Ackroyd incorporates cool blues and greens and other tropical imagery in this label design. Graphics are silkscreened directly to the glass bottles.

● **Champagne** for **Kurpfalz Sektkellerei AG.** Design Firm: **Knut Hartmann Design;** Art Director/Designer/Illustrator: **Knut Hartmann**

This design is properly attired for special occasions and festive celebrations. The bright red band against a warm gray background gives the entire presentation a classy look.

▲ **Autumn Bock Beer** for **Schirf Brewing Company**. Design Firm: **The Weller Institute for the Cure of Design, Inc.;** Art Director/Designer/Illustrator: **Don Weller**

A specialty beer offered in the fall—the traditional season for harvest-time beer fests—Autumn Bock was given a whimsical yet thoroughly German styling.

❖ **Ginebra** for **Bols Argentina, S.A.** Design Firm: **Estudio Hache;** Designers: **Laura Lazzeretti, Marcelo Varela**

The fragrant berries of the juniper—the prime ingredient of gin—provided inspiration for the bright greens and yellows of the Ginebra label.

▲

❖

for **Swan Brewery Co., Ltd**. Design Firm: **Cato Design Inc.;** Designers: **Cato Design Inc.**

A specialty beer produced by Swan, one of Australia's leading breweries, Cockatoo has both a name and a slogan that are thoroughly Australian. The legend, printed at the top of the can, says that the beer was "inspired by the need for refreshment on the little-known tropical island paradise of Australia's west coast—Cockatoo Island."

▲ **The Dufftown, Blair Athol** and **Inchgower** whisky labels for **Bells.** Design Firm: **Michael Peters + Partners;** Art Director/ Designer: **Glenn Tutssel;** Illustrators: **Liz Pyle, Roy Knipe**

Three different malt whiskys, three different marketing strategies. There's a lot to be learned from the varied use of type and color. The black and gold tones of the center label are particularly compelling.

❖ **Rainier** beer packaging for **G. Heileman Brewing Company, Inc. U.S.A.** Design Firm: **Cato Design Inc.;** Designers: **Cato Design Inc.**

Designers consider themselves fortunate when something interesting can be done with the product name. The tableaux of a mountain range clearly identifies Mt. Rainier in Washington state, where the beer is brewed. The letter "R"—rendered in an elegant serif typeface—takes center stage.

▲

❖

■ **Mc Cauls Stout Bier** for **Binding Brauerei AG.** Design Firm: **Knut Hartmann Design;** Art Director: **Roland Mehler;** Designers: **Angelika Rüsseler, Roland Mehler;** Illustrator: **Roland Mehler**

The use of earthy colors, a gold foil neck wrapper and shadow type clearly convey that this is a traditionally brewed Irish stout.

● **Maxim Light Low-Alcohol Bitters** for **Vaux Breweries.** Design Firm: **Graphic Partners;** Designer: **Douglas Alexander**

Maxim Light is one of the United Kingdom's first low-alcohol bitters, produced by Vaux Breweries, the country's second largest independent brewer. Red, white and gold illustrate that this is a "light" libation; gold circle, stripes and foil neck band with a red chevron mark convey sophistication. Printed in three colors on machine-coated stock. The gold was printed twice to add dimension to the color.

☆ **Sambuca Molinari** for **Whitbread N.A.** Design Firm: **Mittleman/Robinson Design Associates;** Designer: **Fred Mittleman**

This is a stunning label design for the number one Sambuca in Italy. The assignment called for a design that said "Italian," high quality, distinctive, elegant. High-contrast colors against a transparent bottle with engraved vertical lines does the job.

▲ **Mango Passion** for **Schieffelin & Somerset Co.** Design Firm: **Mittleman/Robinson Design Associates;** Designer: **Fred Mittleman**

For a new line of Marie Brizzard tropical liqueurs, Mittleman/Robinson chose bright, saturated colors appropriate to the sunny imagery requested by the client. The product—packaged in an existing glass bottle—serves as an equally bright backdrop to the labels.

❖ **Calistoga Lager** for **The Napa Valley Brewing Co.** Design Firm: **Colonna, Farrell: Strategic Marketing & Design;** Art Director: **Ralph Colonna;** Designer: **Amy Racina;** Illustrator: **Mike Gray**

The Napa Valley is renowned for its wineries, but is virtually unknown as a beer-producing region. Still, the association with alcoholic beverages, and its deserved reputation for clean air and water, would seem to augur well for a local beer. Calistoga is a well-known Napa Valley locale, making its name an excellent focal point for the label.

■ **Rathskeller Beer** for **All-American Rathskeller.** Design Firm: **Lanny Sommese Design;** Designer: **Lanny Sommese**

While California micro-breweries strive to forge an identity with new products, Pennsylvania has been famous for its small-run breweries for years: Rolling Rock, Pittsburgh's Iron City and more recently Philadelphia's Dock Street have all garnered rabidly loyal fans. The All-American Rathskeller in State College, home of Penn State University, wanted its private-label beer to both live up to this regional heritage and capitalize on the city's main media property: Penn State's athletic teams. Lanny Sommese chose the university's mascot, the Nittany Lion (a mountain lion named for the nearby Nittany Mountains) as the focal point for this can, printed in three colors on gray aluminum cans.

● **Cascade Premium Lager** for **Cascade Brewery Company.** Design Firm: **Cato Design Inc.;** Designers: **Cato Design Inc.**

A pair of Tasmanian tigers—which are actually wolves—is the focus of the label for Cascade, brewed in Tasmania, Australia. Although semi-mythical in America, in the Pacific, Tasmania is known as a rugged but beautiful land with an unspoiled environment. The Cascade name suggests roaring streams of fresh, pure water—a good image for any beer.

▲ **Dogbolter Beer** for **Matilda Bay Brewery**. Design Firm: **Primo Angeli Inc.;** Creative Director: **Primo Angeli;** Designers: **Carlo Pagoda, Doug Hardenburgh**

Although it has been in business for just half a decade, Matilda Bay of Australia wanted the graphics for its new specialty brew, Dogbolter, to convince drinkers that it delivers "traditional Australian flavor." Dogbolter has a higher alcohol content than most Australian beers, so the brewer also wanted it to look masculine, suggesting it as a libation for those with a strong palate.

❖ **Lone Star** and **Lone Star Light** beers for **G. Heileman Brewing Company, Inc. U.S.A.** Design Firm: **Cato Design Inc.;** Designers: **Cato Design Inc.**

It may be hard to picture Lone Star beer—the homegrown pride of what many residents still call the Republic of Texas—getting its graphics from a studio halfway around the globe. But if the Texas attitude has a sibling anywhere in the world, it is the fierce independence of Australia, home of Cato Design Inc. The illustrations of wildlife and the predominantly white color scheme manage to project a rugged image without falling into the clichéd, over-decorated "Western" look sometimes seen on native products of the American West.

■ **Brooklyn Brewery Lager** for **Brooklyn Brewery**. Design Firm: **Milton Glaser, Inc.;** Art Director/Designer: **Milton Glaser**

Brooklyn, New York has always taken pride in having its own identity despite being cheek-by-jowl with the Manhattan megalopolis. The big "B" logo capitalizes on that sentiment and recalls the days when the Dodgers were the Brooklyn Dodgers and Moxie was the soda of choice.

▲ **Lamot Pils Lager** for **Bass.** Design Firm: **Michael Peters + Partners;** Art Director/Designer: **Karen Welman**

This lager isn't just smooth, it's "seriously smooth"—and hearty. The graphics aren't quite as serious as the brew; there are wavy lines inside the block-style letters of the product name, and another set of curved lines in the crest-style graphic that forms a background to the logo treatment.

❖ **Bacardi Breezer** for **Bacardi Imports, Inc.;** Design Firm: **Congdon Macdonald Inc.;** Art Director: **Roger Davidoff;** Designers: **Arthur Congdon, Roger Davidoff, Barbara Tocchet, Patrina Marino, Constance Venable**

This line of rum refreshers needed to carry on the Bacardi Light Rum heritage and convey the traditional look of a quality alcoholic beverage. Vivid four-color photographs capture the refreshing tastes of the various juice and rum combinations, while the white background communicates that these beverages are lighter in taste than rum. The labels are printed offset in six colors on foil stock; the carrier is printed using four-color process, matched gold, and varnish.

Eureka California Lager for **Los Angeles Brewing Company, Inc.** Design Firm: **Bright & Associates;** Art Directors: **Keith Bright, Barbara Eadie Myer, Raymond Wood;** Designer: **Barbara Eadie Myer;** Illustrator: **Raymond Wood**

The Los Angeles Brewing Company Inc. concocted this traditional European Lager with the beer connoisseur in mind. Bright & Associates was commissioned to create a memorable name that would convey the regional heritage of the product. At the same time, the brewery wanted a unique and identifiable packaging design system that projected a classic yet contemporary image of uncompromising freshness, taste and quality. The labels are printed in five colors on 45-pound white coated label stock with a varnish.

▲ **Wicked Ale** for **Pete's Brewing Co.** Design Firm: **Primo Angeli Inc.;** Creative Director: **Primo Angeli;** Designers: **Doug Hardenburgh, Kelly O'Kane**

Pete's Brewing Co., a Palo Alto, California-based micro-brewery, had a great product and a great name but its label projected a so-so image. The brewery's owner, Pete, is known as a maverick in the beer industry, so it seemed natural to call his product "Wicked Ale." Research showed great consumer sympathy for the rascality implied by the name. The graphics were developed to support the notions that this brew is just a little bit "bad" and that Pete lavishes the kind of expense and effort on it that the major brewers can't afford.

❖ **Park City Shakespeare Beare** for **Park City Shakespeare Festival.** Design Firm: **The Weller Institute for the Cure of Design, Inc.;** Art Director/Designer/Illustrator: **Don Weller**

Designed exclusively for sale at a summertime outdoor Shakespeare festival, the label for this Beare had to look fun and refreshing without costing a fortune to produce. The answer was to use the Bard's own face and print one color on colored stock.

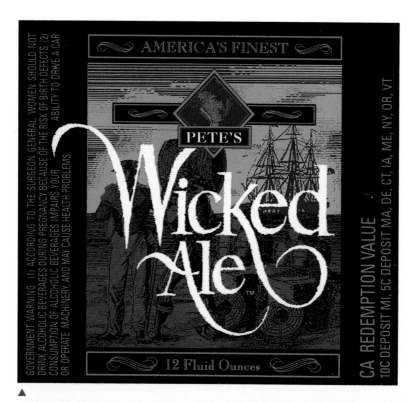

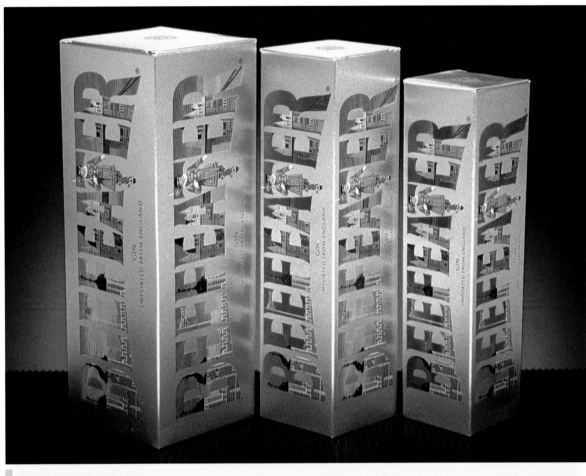

■ **Beefeater Gin** for **Buckingham Wile Co**. Design Firm: **Mittleman/Robinson Design Associates**; Art Director: **Fred Mittleman**; Illustrator: **John Styga**

A London scene is viewed through the world-famous Beefeater logo on all four panels of this gift box. The illustration on each panel is keyed in a different color to suggest morning, midday, sundown and night. The box was developed primarily as a Christmas gift package, but with a look that outlives the holidays.

● **Fine Fare Dark Rum** for **Fine Fare**. Design Firm: **Michael Peters + Partners**; Art Director/Designer: **Glenn Tutssel**; Illustrator: **Rory Kee**

Rum and the British navy are ingrained in our minds as a natural pair. The British tar with his daily ration of grog carried the day for Nelson at Trafalgar and for Admiral Tovey, whose crews sank the battleship Bismarck in 1941. Playing on this association, the designers used naval flags to spell out "Fine Fare" on the front label and as decorative elements on the rear.

▲ **Castlemaine Dry** for **Bond Brewing.** Design Firm: **Cato Design Inc.;** Designers: **Cato Design Inc.**

Dry beers are all the rage this year. Australia-based Bond Brewing asked for a label that would convey the idea of lighter taste without compromising the notion that the brew is refreshing. An eagle, one of the beer-drinking world's most popular symbols, provides the association with full-bodied taste and the State of Queensland.

❖ **Swan Dry** for **Bond Brewing.** Design Firm: **Cato Design Inc.;** Designers: **Cato Design Inc.**

Anyone can make a dry beer, but not everyone has the huge equity that Bond Brewery has in its trademark outline of a swan. The focus of this label for the first dry beer in Australia was almost automatic; the designers have used the word dry very large to instantly distinguish the product from its many siblings in Swan's extensive line.

■ **Loburg Beer** for **Interbrew Belgium.** Design Firm: **Design Board Behaeghel & Partners** Art Director: **Denis Keller;** Designer/Illustrator: **Thierry Borremans**

A classic bottle shape and bold typography distinguish Loburg as a premium brew, an effect hard to achieve in Belgium, which boasts gourmet breweries that have been making tiny—and expensive—batches of beer for centuries.

● **Hunde Beer** for **Robyn Brewery**. Design Firm: **Frazier Design;** Art Director/Illustrator: **Craig Frazier;** Designers: **Craig Frazier, Grant Peterson;** Photographer: **Jock McDonald**

Photographs are used on beer labels only very rarely. This one is a refreshing change of pace, offering not only a photo but an unusual color palette—green—to instantly grab attention. The soulful dachshund is really too cute for words, and the label copy makes the most of the illustration, calling Hunde a "Full Pedigreed Brew" and averring that it is "Light, Long and Low."

HEALTH & BEAUTY

Fashion has long set the pattern for product graphics in the upper reaches of the health and beauty market. That trend now extends down to the most basic products: soaps, cotton swabs, tissues, creams. Excepting medicines, communicating product benefits is out and projecting an upscale image is becoming the main requirement for the packaging of personal products.

This may forecast a changing role for product graphics in this category. In the U.S., marketers seem to be relying more on advertising to communicate product benefits. The packaging has become an extension of the product, adding value to the basic commodity. Soap pakaging displayed on a countertop instead of concealed in a cabinet must harmonize with both the decor of the powder room and the esthetic tastes of the buyer. Japanese designers have been using this approach for years, conceiving packages as pure art, with minimal copy.

The same can be said of soft soaps, tissues, and even items not usually left out in view such as hygiene products. Consumers seem to be saying that what they buy is a reflection of who they are and how they feel about themselves. This makes the most mundane products a personal signature. They now require an elegance and sophistication of image that was formerly reserved for designer fragrances.♦

Just looking at graphics and containers alone, it's sometimes difficult to tell whether health and beauty aids are intended for sale in a supermarket or in a boutique for the super-rich.

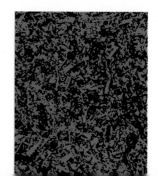

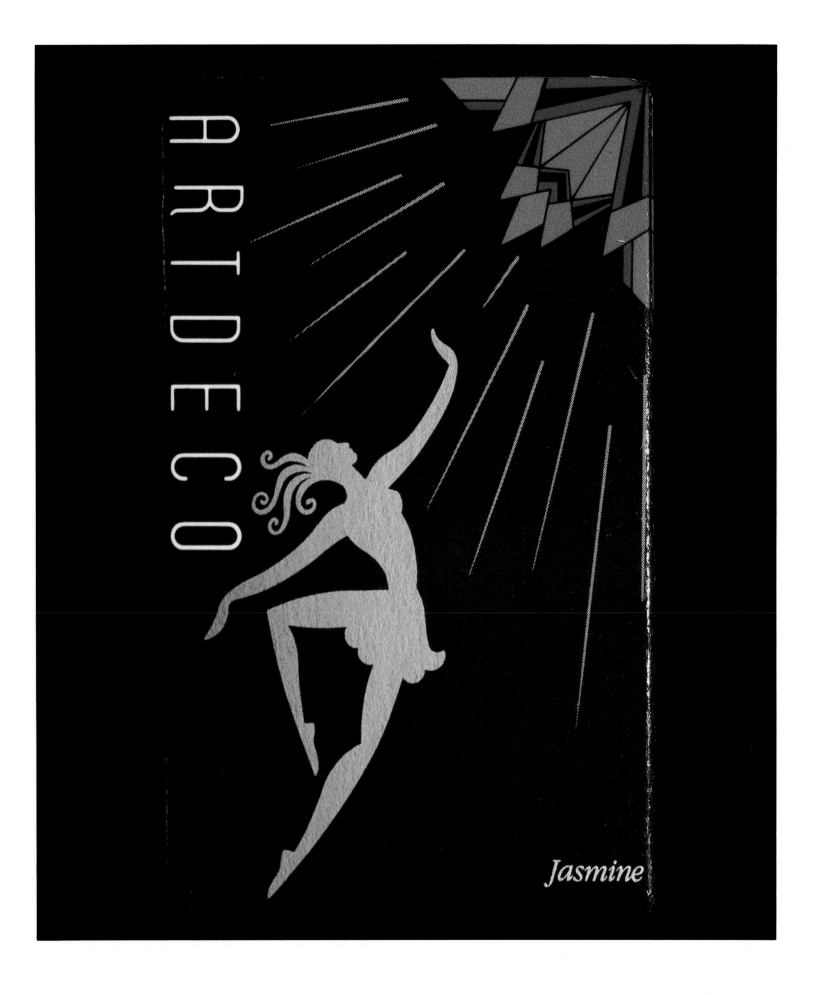

▲ **Winceramy** for **Kanebo Co**. Design Firm: **Shigeru Akizuki;** Art Director: **Shigeru Akizuki;** Designers: **Shigeru Akizuki, Mayumi Iwakiri**

This collection of winter cosmetics is an extension to the Ceramy line. The characters and patterns are embossed on a matte background.

❖ **Ceramy** for **Kanebo Co**. Design Firm: **Shigeru Akizuki;** Art Director/Designer: **Shigeru Akizuki**

These packages show the wide range of graphics developed for Ceramy foundation products. In keeping with the tastes of its young buyers, the visual images are bright and eclectic.

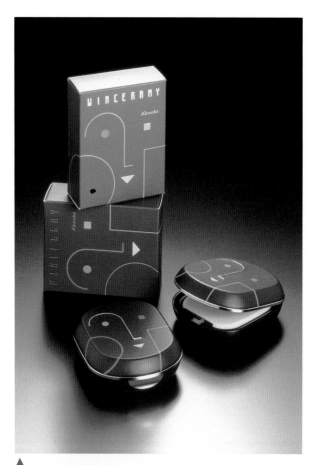

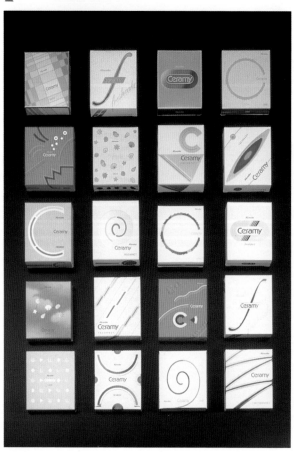

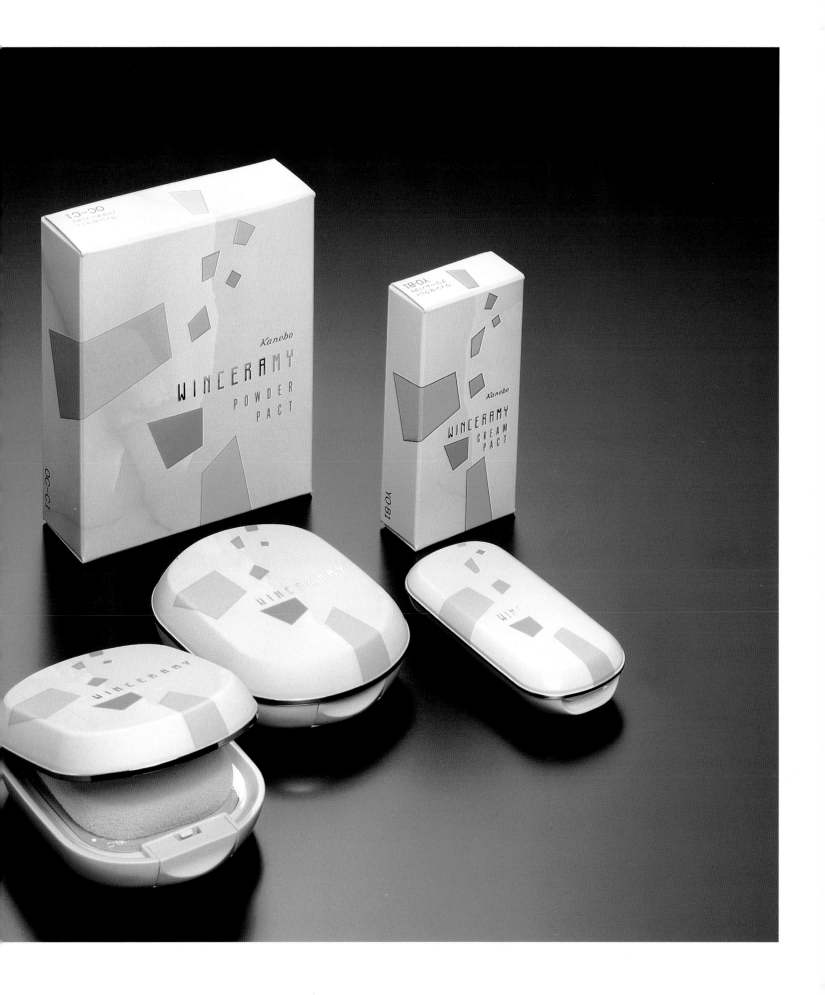

▲ **Art Deco** soaps for **Gianna Company, Limited.** Design Firm: **Alan Chan Design Company;** Art Director: **Alan Chan;** Designers: **Alan Chan, Alvin Chan, Phillip Leung**

The Jazz Age lives on in these Erté-influenced graphics for Art Deco soap. The use of metallic colors for both varieties featured on this spread successfully evokes the brass-and-glass images that typify the era.

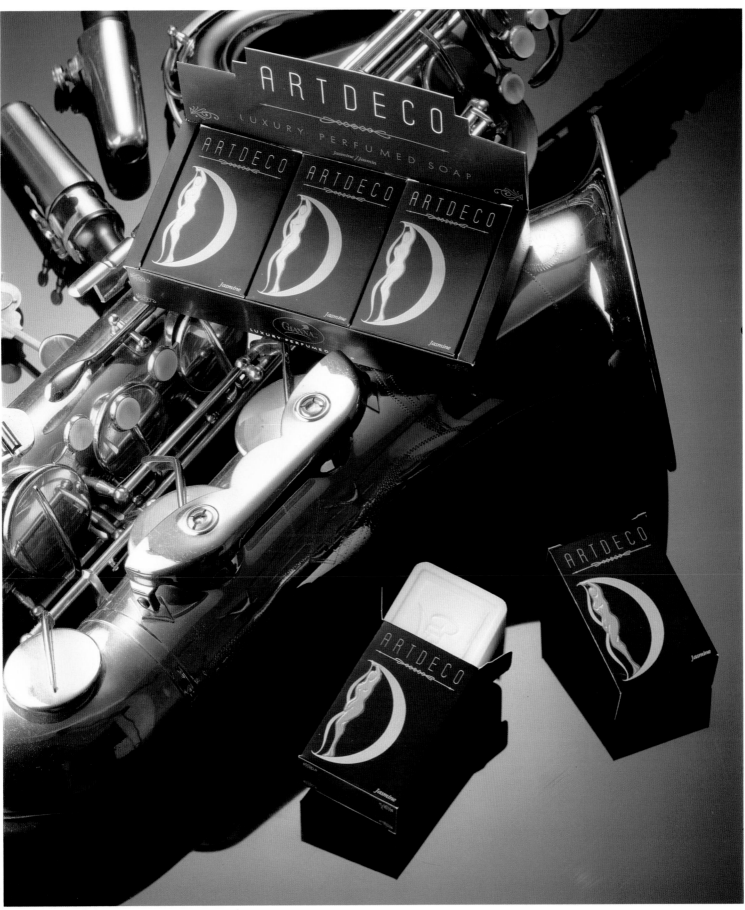

▲ **Pinstripe Hotel Amenities** for **Procter & Gamble Company.** Design Firm: **Libby Perszyk Kathman;** Art Director: **Dutro Blocksam;** Designer: **Liz Kathman Grubow**

Packaging for The Pinstripe Collection of hotel amenities was designed to look distinctive in a variety of hotel decors. The design is carried out in three different colors—off-white, gray and black (page 187)—to match a variety of hotel room decorating schemes.

❖ **Softsoap Pastels** for **Softsoap Inc.** Design Firm: **Hillis Mackey & Company;** Art Director/Designer: **Liz Schupanitz;** Illustrator: **Gary Kelly**

Hillis Mackey solved a common dilemma for consumers who want a soft soap container that looks elegant and classy—not country bumpkin (how many illustrations of ducks and cows can consumers possibly stand?). The floral pattern of soft, contemporary colors is enhanced by the use of gold foil.

■ Soap packaging for **Gianna Company Limited.** Design Firm: **Alan Chan Design Company;** Art Director: **Alan Chan;** Designers: **Alan Chan, Alvin Chan, Phillip Leung**

Another design for Gianna Company Limited, this packaging draws on Oriental imagery to project an upscale image.

● Hotels amenities for **Hyatt Hotels.** Design Firm: **Primo Angeli Inc.;** Creative Director: **Primo Angeli;** Designers: **Ray Honda, Ian McLean, Doug Hardenburgh**

A silent battle has been going on in the hotel industry for about ten years. It's called the amenities war, and it's fought with one-ounce bottles of shampoo, conditioner and other bodycare items. Hyatt Hotels, which pioneered the concept of amenities, hired Primo Angeli Inc. to devise two new identity systems—one for its Regency hotels, the other for Hyatt Resort Hotels—that could be adapted to more than 40 items ranging from shampoo to shirt valets. Featured is the packaging for the Resort hotels. It was originally designed in a gray-on-gray pattern, but the client decided that a white-on-white color scheme would be better suited to a Resort hotel. Pastel color bands distinguish the various products.

▲ **Ceramy** cosmetics for **Kanebo Co.** Design Firm: **Shigeru Akizuki;** Art Director: **Shigeru Akizuki;** Designers: **Shigeru Akizuki, Mayumi Iwakiri**

Shigeru Akizuki demonstrates the versatility of its designers with these three package designs for Ceramy cosmetics. The Ceramy line includes numerous items in a wide range of product categories, making the assignment to both unify and differentiate the individual items a difficult one. The designers have maintained continuity in the line by using bright colors and fresh, outdoor imagery.

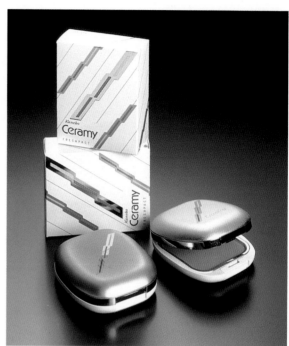

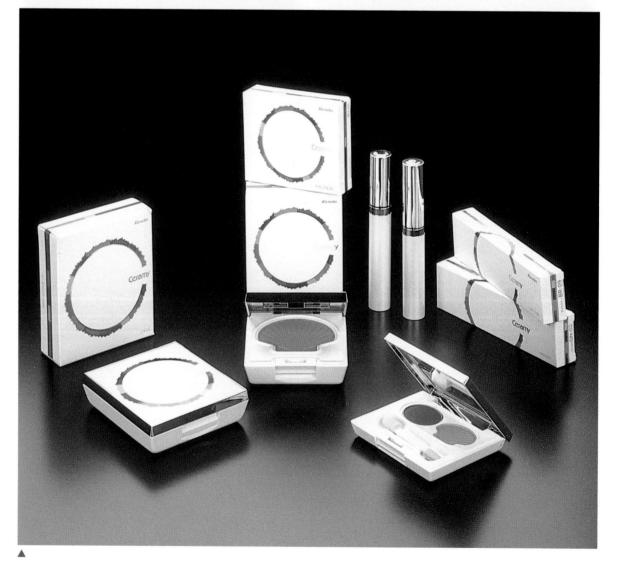

❖ **SensiBelle Cosmetics** for **Chesebrough-Pond's Inc.** Design Firm: **Hans Flink Design Inc.;** Art Directors: **Hans D. Flink, Ron Vandenberg;** Designers: **Hans Flink Design staff**

SensiBelle is a line of cosmetics for sensitive skin sold in Germany. A serious brand image is given friendly overtones through the use of subtle floral touches and hot stamping.

▪ **Hoi Tong Talcum Powder** for **Sam Fong Cosmetic Co. Ltd.** Design Firm: **Alan Chan Design Company;** Art Director: **Alan Chan;** Designers: **Alan Chan, Andy Ip**

This soft and silky powder is handmade from the finest natural ingredients according to an ancient Chinese formula. A picture of a woman with porcelain-like skin illustrates the benefits of this natural product.

▲ **Windsor Hotel Amenities** for **Procter & Gamble.** Design Firm: **Libby Perszyk Kathman;** Art Director: **Dutro Blocksam;** Designer: **Iko Lin;** Illustrator: **Bill Ellison**

The Windsor Collection of hotel amenities offers a complete range of Procter & Gamble products including Oil of Olay and Pantene. Gold foil stamping on a marbleized background gives these products a look that's elegant enough for a luxury hotel.

❖ Soap packaging for **Gianna Company Limited.** Design Firm: **Alan Chan Design Company;** Art Director: **Alan Chan;** Designers: **Alan Chan, Alvin Chan, Phillip Leung**

Traditional prints provide the perfect background for these soap packages. The intimate scenes suggest privacy and hint at romance—the perfect combination for a luxury cosmetic product.

▲

❖

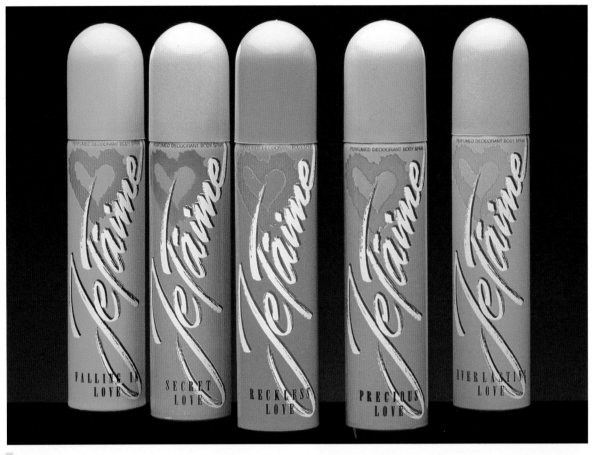

■ **Je T'aime** deodorant. Design Firm: **Pentagraph;** Art Director/ Designer: **Mark Posnett**

Je T'aime (French for "I love you") is a line of deodorants for teenage girls. Each fragrance is specially formulated for a different kind of love; for example, the blue package in the center is for "Reckless Love." A fun package design for a market that thrives on novelty.

● **Perfume** for **Kanebo Co.** Art Director/Designer: **Shigeru Akizuki**

"Shiran," the Japanese word for purple orchid, is symbolized by a splash of purple behind a highly-stylized abstract drawing. The Oriental patterns are embossed on a matte varnish paper.

☆ Soap packaging for **Gianna Company Limited.** Design Firm: **Alan Chan Design Company;** Art Director: **Alan Chan;** Designers: **Alan Chan, Alvin Chan, Phillip Leung**

The porcelain-like skin of the woman in the portrait helps consumers make the connection between Gianna soap's elegant wrapping and its more basic function.

▲ **Browns Millefleurs** scented gift items for **Austin Morgan & Co. Pty. Ltd.** Design Firm: **Andrew Bell Graphic Partners;** Designer: **Andrew Bell;** Illustrators: **Susan Morris, Selwyn Slaney**

A medley of pastel colors in a pretty floral design impart a look of elegance to this selection of scented products, including drawer liners, soap, lotion and bath gel.

❖ Cologne packaging for **Gendarme.** Design Firm: **Stan Evenson Design;** Art Director/Designer: **Stan Evenson**

Stan Evenson Design was commissioned to develop a strong and distinctive logo for this men's cologne without benefit of a large budget. A swash was placed beneath the logo to symbolize a refreshing splash of the fragrance.

■ **Natural Impressions** beauty aids for **Shaklee Corporation.** Design Firm: **Primo Angeli, Inc.;** Creative Director: **Primo Angeli;** Designers: **Vicky Cero, Ian McLean**

This line of health products is not sold at retail; it's sold directly to consumers by Shaklee representatives and through mail catalogs. The products—which include a moisture cream, cleansing bar and skin tonic—were built around a "beauty recovery complex" formulated to minimize lines and wrinkles.

▲

❖

■

● Soap packaging for **Gianna Company Limited.** Design Firm: **Alan Chan Design Company;** Art Director: **Alan Chan;** Designers: **Alan Chan, Alvin Chan, Phillip Leung**

Alan Chan Design has done a terrific job of distinguishing the many products in the Gianna soap line. The use of a variety of styles and color schemes —rather than a unified, family-wide approach—is unusual. In this case, it seems to work well, creating a range of looks and moods to suit almost everyone.

▲ **The Repair Kit** for **Dash Products, Inc**. Design Firm: **American Design;** Art Director: **Allen Haeger;** Designers: **Harold Maurer, Jill Finche-Graham**

A departure from the fields-of-wheat-all-natural-goodness style of graphics usually seen on nutritional products, The Repair Kit looks more like something that belongs in the automotive section. The unusual shape and graphics combine to create a look that is in no danger of quietly blending into any retail shelf.

❖ Vitamins for **Pioneer, Inc**. Design Firm: **American Design;** Art Director: **Allen Haeger;** Designer: **Harold Maurer**

This more traditional approach to nutritional supplements, also by American Design, was a response to the client's desire for an elegant, two-color label.

■ Liquid supplements for **Real Life Research, Inc**. Design Firm: **American Design;** Art Director: **Allen Haeger;** Designer: **Harold Maurer;** Photographer: **David Sharpe**

To introduce a different kind of nutritional supplement—a liquid placed under the tongue—American Design created an ultra-modern, clean-and-clinical style and packaged it in an eye-catching counter display.

▲

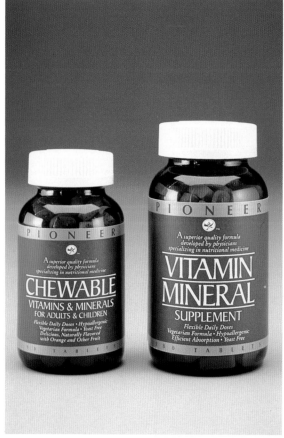

❖   ■

● **Prescripta** for **New Mood Pre-scripta**. Design Firm: **Graphic Partners;** Art Director/Designer: **Ron Burnett;** Illustrator: **Jacqueline Watt**

An authoritative–but not clinical—look was needed for this line of ten multi-nutrient products. The design combines classical Greek figures with strong typography and the detailed product information needed to properly convey product usage and promises to the consumer. Prescripta was awarded a Clio in the international OTC division in 1989.

☆ Drug packaging for **Bagó Laboratories**. Art Director/Designer: **Eduardo Cánovas**

Bagó Laboratories, a large Argentinian pharmaceutical firm, commissioned a series of packages to be used to promote its products to physicians as well as new packaging for its line of anti-diarrheal products.

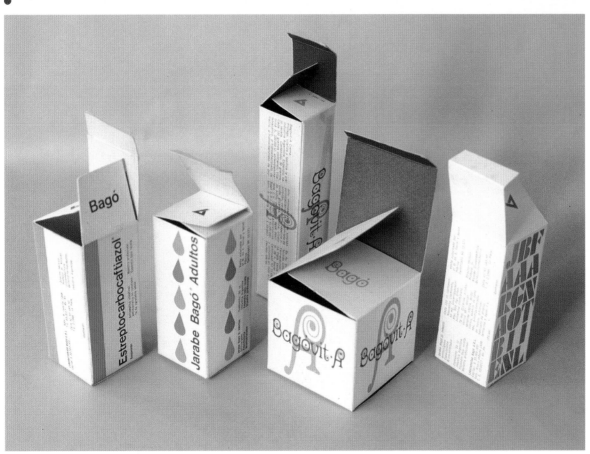

▲ **Obiron** for **Pfizer Pty. Ltd**. Design Firm: **Raymond Bennett Design;** Art Director/Designer: **Raymond Bennett**

A clinical, yet friendly and up-beat look characterizes these Obiron packages created by Raymond Bennett for the Australian division of Pfizer. The use of informal graphics—the free-floating shapes and primary colors—contrasts nicely with the sterile look of many products in this category.

❖ **Iso Multi-Vitamin** for **Isotek.** Design Firm: **The Thompson Design Group;** Art Director: **Dennis Thompson;** Designers: **Dennis Thompson, Veronica Denny**

This die-cut box, printed five colors plus varnish on 12-point stock, has a lid which folds up to act as a header card for one-at-a-time sales of the foil-packed tablets.

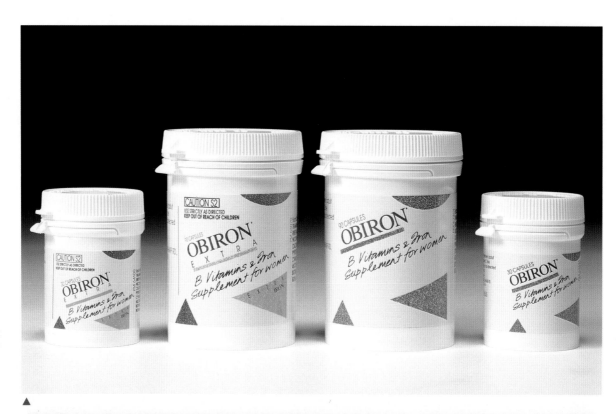

▲

❖

Sinex for **Richardson-Vicks**. Design Firm: **Hans Flink Design Inc.;** Art Directors: **Hans D. Flink, Kathie Haffner;** Designers: **Hans Flink Design staff**

When Richardson-Vicks introduced a new dispenser for its Sinex nasal spray, Hans Flink Design chose to focus buyers' attention on the benefit: a much finer spray than that delivered by ordinary squeeze bottles. An airbrush illustration of the atomizer, positioned to overlap the product name slightly, creates an illusion of three dimensions.

▲ **New Palmolive Hypo-Allergenic Soap** for **Colgate-Palmolive.** Design Firm: **Joel Bronz Design;** Designer: **Karen Willoughby**

This new inexpensive hypo-allergenic soap had to compete with many well-known and long-established hypo-allergenic brands. The Palmolive name was the product's biggest asset, so Joel Bronz Design featured it prominently. The blue-and-white color scheme and contemporary graphics appeal to the health-conscious target audience. Printed three colors on white paper with a varnish.

❖ **Camay Canada** for **Procter & Gamble.** Design Firm: **Libby Perszyk Kathman;** Art Director: **Marjorie Carleton;** Designer: **John Metz**

These soap cartons were designed to convey a fresh, youthful vitality with the confidence of a well-known brand.

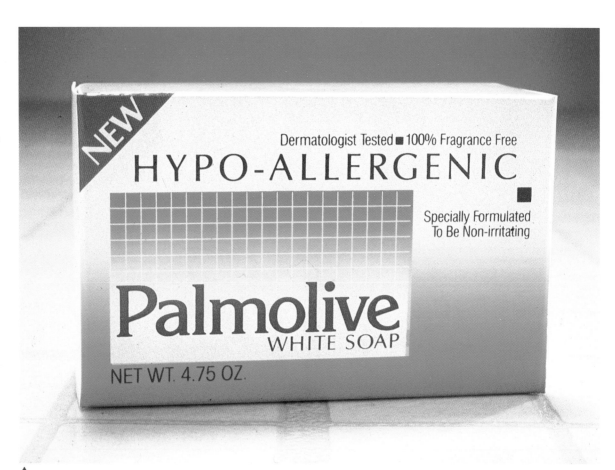

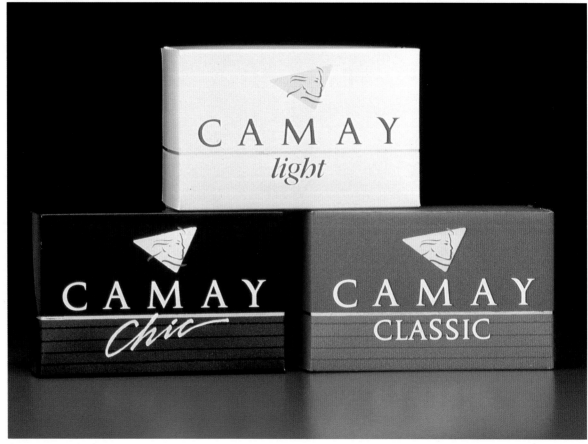

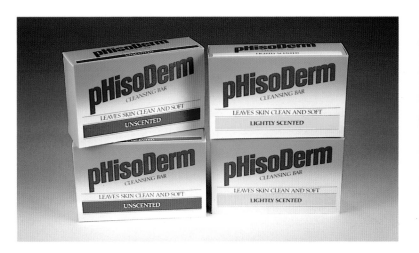

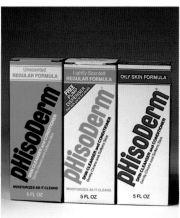

pHisoDerm for **Winthrop Consumer Products.** Design Firm: **Hans Flink Design Inc.;** Art Director: **Hans D. Flink;** Designers: **Hans Flink Design staff**

Consumers have long known pHisoDerm by its distinctive green packaging (upper right). In updating the package, Hans Flink Design retained the color but softened the overall impression by having the green fade into white. A change in typeface and color band placement completes the new look.

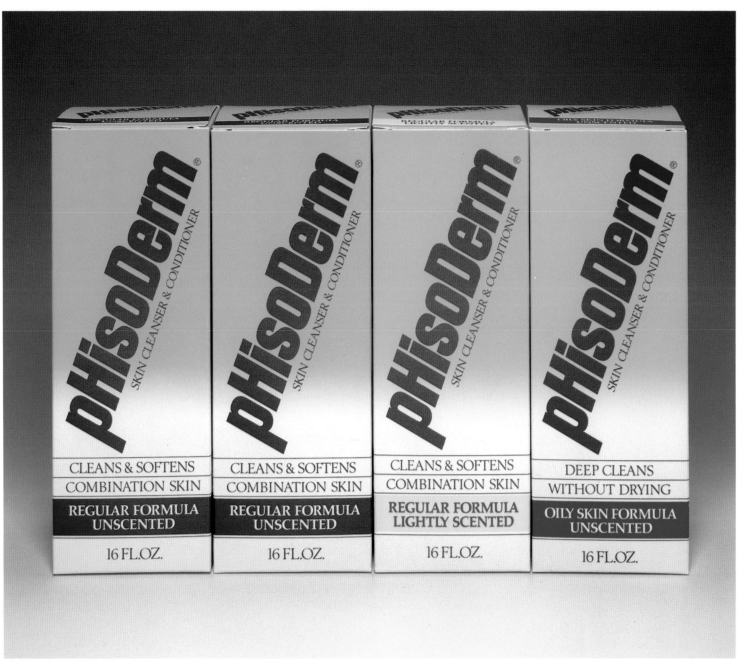

▲ **Buf Puf Cleanser** for **3M Corp**. Design Firm: **Peterson & Blyth;** Art Directors: **John Blyth, Barbara Wentz;** Designer: **Barbara Wentz**

The colors and graphics of this extension to 3M's Buf Puf line project gentleness; one of consumers' top concerns about facial products is that they not be harsh or harmful to their skin.

❖ **Asda Extra-Strength Tissues** for **Asda Stores, Ltd.** Design Firm: **Elmwood Design Ltd.;** Designer/Illustrator: **Clare Walker**

Most tissue packages are all pastels, butterflies and flowers. But Asda Stores wanted customers to know that its private label tissues are bigger, thicker and stronger than ordinary tissues, so Elmwood Design combined an elephant—a traditional symbol of brute size and strength—with hard-edged geometric shapes in a variety of saturated colors.

▲

❖

■ **Soft & Dri Antiperspirant** for **The Gillette Company.** Design Firm: **Wallace Church Associates, Inc.;** Art Directors: **Stanley Church, Robert Wallace;** Designers: **Melissa Smith-Hazen, Angela Valenti;** Illustrator: **Joyce Kitchell;** Typographic Design: **Angela Valenti, Taro Yamashita**

A successful brand for more than a decade, Soft & Dri was losing market share. To help arrest the decline, The Gillette Company commissioned a total overhaul of the brand's graphic identity. The ad hoc program, worked out piecemeal as line extensions were introduced over the years, was replaced with an overall floral theme, keying each product to a color embodied in a stylized flower.

● **Johnson's Swabs** for **Johnson & Johnson**. Design Firm: **Apple Design Source, Inc.;** Designers: **Monica Kurkemelis, Nancy Brogden**

Cotton swabs—once used for limited and specific cleaning chores—have become a ubiquitous bath accessory. These containers, available in several color schemes to match a variety of decors, are designed to make consumers feel good about bringing their swabs out of the closet and onto the bathroom counter where they are handier and more likely to be used.

▲ **Moisture Soaps** for **Kiss My Face Corporation.** Design Firm: **Alternatives;** Art Director/Designer: **Julie Koch-Beinke**

This line of moisture soaps was developed as a bridge between the company's successful soap products and moisturizers. The graphics clearly communicate the company's fun image within the industry. The colors are bold enough to stand out on a crowded retail shelf, but coordinate well with other Kiss My Face products. PVC label with UV sealer printed two color.

❖ **Honey & Calendula Moisturizer** for **Kiss My Face Corporation.** Design Firm: **Alternatives;** Art Director: **Julie Koch-Beinke;** Designer: **Kevin Yates**

Extra dry skin is a serious problem, but the designers bring a cheerful note to the subject with playful graphics and bright colors. The honeycomb background pattern symbolizes the moisturizing properties of honey and calendula.

✩ **Prell Shampoo** and **Conditioner** for **Procter & Gamble.** Design Firm: **Libby Perszyk Kathman;** Art Director: **Ron Zamorski;** Designer: **Liz Kathman Grubow**

The old Prell Shampoo packaging was the easiest to locate in the shampoo section—just look for the green liquid in the transparent bottle. Libby Perszyk Kathman was challenged to develop a new look for Prell products that would project a more contemporary image without sacrificing elements of the old familiar packaging.

▲

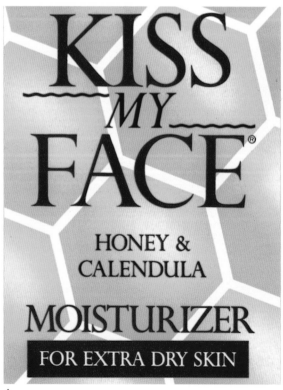

❖

■

● **Carefree** for **Johnson & Johnson's Personal Products division.** Design Firm: **Peterson & Blyth;** Art Directors: **Ronald Peterson, David Scarlett;** Designer: **Jacquie Fauter-MacConnell**

New packaging for Carefree was given a more dynamic look to appeal to today's active working woman. Bright colors and bold graphics heighten shelf impact and visibility—attributes that are vital to stimulating impulse sales.

☆ **Sure & Natural** for **Johnson & Johnson Personal Products Division.** Design Firm: **Peterson & Blyth;** Art Directors: **Ronald Peterson, David Scarlett;** Designer: **Janeen Geary**

A stylish, more sophisticated look was achieved with the use of pastels colors—shaded in some areas—and an elegant italicized typeface for the logo.

▲ **Fidgi** for **Ellebelle PTY Ltd.**
Design Firm: **Pentagraph;** Designer: **Alexis Visser**

These new graphics for Fidgi were created for a range of special Christmas products.

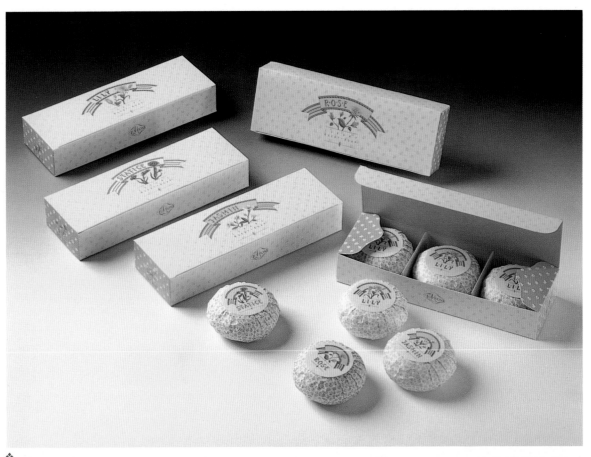

❖ Soap for **Lutex Company Ltd**. Design Firm: **Kan Tai-keung Design & Associates Ltd.;** Art Director: **Kan Tai-keung**; Designer: **Eddy Yu**

This collection of gift soaps for a Hong Kong exporter uses botanical-style illustrations to good advantage.

■ **Sixth Sense** for **Beechams South Africa**. Design Firm: **Pentagraph;** Designers: **Pentagraph Design Team;** Industrial Design: **Kees Schilperoort**

Sixth Sense is a range of deodorants aimed primarily at teenagers and young adults. Each fragrance promises to handle a variety of emotions and is duly illustrated—for example, a crescent-shaped moon for "dreamy feelings," a heart for "loving feelings."

▲ **Kayser** stockings for **Australian Consolidated Hosiery.** Design Firm: **Cato Design Inc.;** Designers: **Cato Design Inc.**

The gray marbleized textured background selected for these Australian stockings makes a sophisticated presentation in the hosiery section of fine department stores.

❖ **Sfera** perfume for **Sfera.** Design Firm: **Michael Peters + Partners;** Art Director/Designer: **Roger Ackroyd**

An unusual name and elegant graphics prove to be a winning combination for this perfume. Elements are silkscreened onto the frosted bottle.

Circe beauty products for **Wallace International Ltd., Australia.** Design Firm: **Cato Design Inc.;** Designers: **Cato Design Inc.**

An exclusive range of skin care products containing seaweed, Circe is sold only through direct mail. The name relates to the mythical Greek sea goddess, the enchantress.

CONSUMER GOODS

Perhaps the biggest swing in the field of product graphics may have occurred in consumer goods. The category was a bastion of conservatism, and as such, represents a huge backlog of under-designed packaging.

Clients have come out swinging, however, and the results are impressive. Efforts to put their best foot forward visually are evident in the graphics for such products as Stride-Rite shoes and LA Gear sneakers (both featured in this chapter).

To an extent, the continuously rising visual ante required to get into a consumer goods category is a spillover from the hyper-competitive arena of food packaging. Good design can mean the difference between a retailer granting a new product two facings or no facings at all. The phenomenon is known to psychologists as "velocitization." After you've been in a car going sixty miles per hour for half a day, you hardly feel as though you're moving. You become accustomed to the speed. Consumers have undergone "velocitization" with respect to visual communications. They no longer respond to messages—advertisements or products on a shelf—unless their appearance is compelling, packed with the kinds of subtle messages that are the result of a deliberate design process. ♦

The growing diversity of attitudes, desires and esthetics among buyers has prompted clients to more clearly appreciate the value of good design in the marketing of consumer goods.

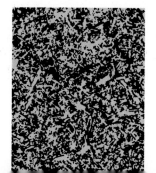

▲ Clothing labels for Dégage. Design Firm: **Hornall Anderson Design Works;** Art Director: **Jack Anderson;** Designers: **Jack Anderson, Julie Tanagi**

Speckletone papers cut in geometric shapes promote Degage as an upscale designer jean in a highly-competitive, brand-driven market.

❖ **Sutter Creek** classic menswear for **Levi Strauss & Co.** Design Firm: **Rene Yung Communications Design Inc.;** Art Director/Designer: **Rene Yung**

A classic line of clothing calls for classic graphics. Rene Yung uses a landscape illustration and rich green and red hues on hang tags, neck labels and merchandising aids.

■ Hang tags for **K2 Corporation.** Design Firm: **Hornall Anderson Design Works;** Art Director: **Jack Anderson;** Designers: **Jack Anderson, Julie Tanagi**

The K2 Corporation wanted a consistent look for three separate lines of clothing without sacrificing brand identity. Different paper stocks and color schemes give each line a distinctive look.

● Swatch box for **Deepa Textiles.** Design Firm: **Gerald Reis & Company;** Art Director: **Gerald Reis;** Designers: **Gerald Reis, Wilson Ong**

The shape of the logo, blind embossed on the oversized labels, signifies soft folds of cloth pierced by a flame. Gold ink and a subtle wash of blue communicate the elegance of the fabrics, while the plain corrugated box covered with handmade paper anchors the identity with a certain earthiness.

▲

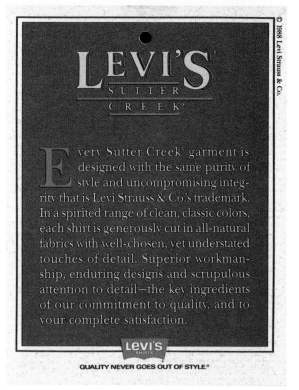

❖

▲ Self-promotional hang tags. Design Firm: **Platinum Design, Inc.;** Art Director: **Victoria Peslak;** Designer: **Sandra Quinn**

Platinum Design uses these highly stylized hang tags in place of mailing labels when sending portfolios to clients. The tag featured at right serves as both a holiday greeting and tree ornament. Both are die-cut and printed in four colors with a varnish.

❖ Hang tags and labels for **Fashion Stores Association.** Design Firm: **WRK, Inc.;** Art Directors/ Designers: **Michelle Knauss, Debbie Robinson**

WRK, Inc. developed the name and designed garment tags for Fashion Stores Association's various clothing lines.

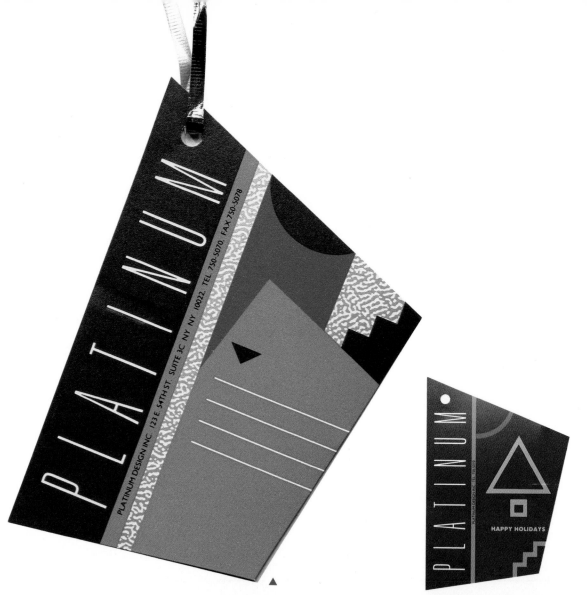

Clothing tags and packaging for **J. Riggings.** Design Firm: **Robert P Gersin Associates;** Art Director: **Scott Bolestridge**

Commissioned to create a new identity for J. Riggings, a chain of clothing stores for young men, Robert P Gersin Associates developed a complete graphics systems (from fixtures to hang tags) around a new logotype. A strong, masculine letterform with squared-off letters proved effective in consumer tests. Photographs show young men dressed in various styles of clothing.

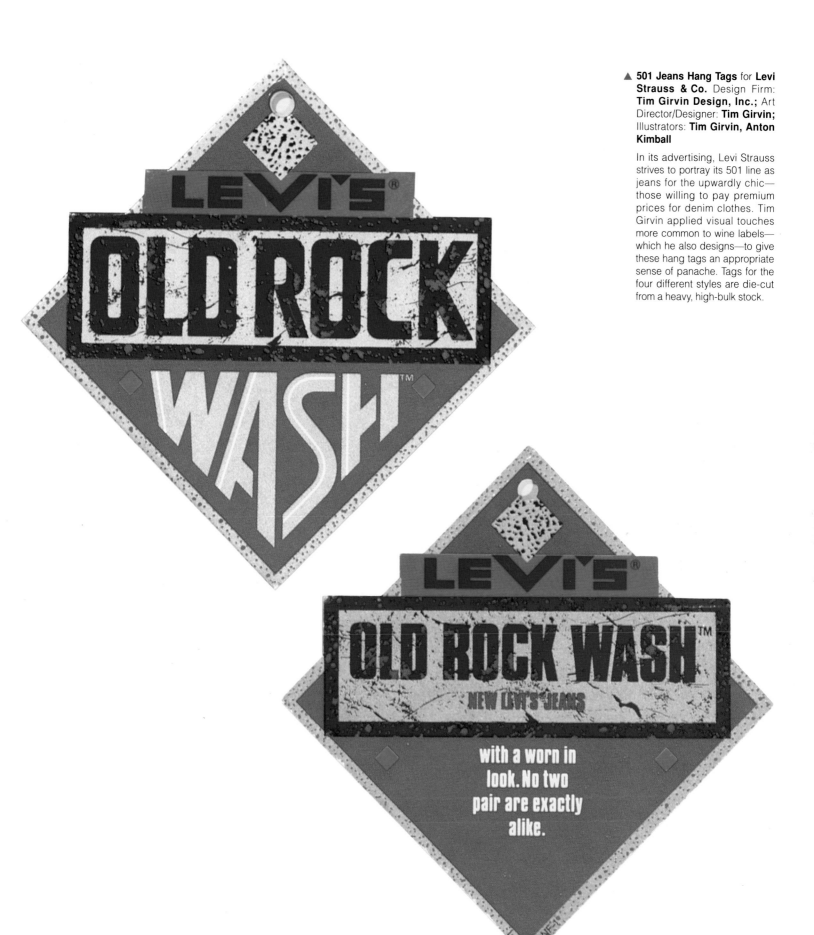

▲ **501 Jeans Hang Tags** for **Levi Strauss & Co.** Design Firm: **Tim Girvin Design, Inc.;** Art Director/Designer: **Tim Girvin;** Illustrators: **Tim Girvin, Anton Kimball**

In its advertising, Levi Strauss strives to portray its 501 line as jeans for the upwardly chic—those willing to pay premium prices for denim clothes. Tim Girvin applied visual touches more common to wine labels—which he also designs—to give these hang tags an appropriate sense of panache. Tags for the four different styles are die-cut from a heavy, high-bulk stock.

▲ Tag and shopping bags for **Cartoon Corner**. Design Firm: **Robert P Gersin Associates;** Art Director: **Robert P Gersin;** Designer: **Joanne Schumacher**

This logotype, inspired by classic cartoon images, was developed for a new chain of specialty stores that sell merchandise which features licensed cartoon characters. The bold letters include a piece of cheese, a lightning bolt and a pair of eyes. The label is printed on pressure-sensitive paper, while the handle bag is printed on plastic and the smaller bag on 70-pound coated paper.

FOR THE KID IN ALL OF US

CARTOON

C O R N E R

Bridgewater Commons   Burlington Mall   Crossgates Mall Holyoke Mall at Ingleside   Pheasant Lane Mall

❖ Tag for **K2 Corporation.** Design Firm: **Hornall Anderson Design Works;** Art Director: **Jack Anderson;** Designers: **Jack Anderson, Julie Tanagi**

Despite the considerable equity K2 has built among outdoor enthusiasts, it asked for a label which would play down the K2 name for its Action Plus line, putting the emphasis instead on a trendy, energetic look.

■ Goose down quilt and pillows for **Arthur Ellis.** Design Firm: **Farman Foley Gill Pty.Ltd.;** Art Director: **Dennis Edlin;** Designer: **Andrew Bell;** Illustrator: **Lena Gan**

This special package combining a quilt and pillows was developed as an all-in-one wedding gift.

● Hang tag for **California Beach Co.** Design Firm: **Tracy Sabin Illustration & Design;** Art Director: **Richard Sawyer;** Illustrator: **Tracy Sabin**

The prime market for California Beach Company's sportswear is teenage boys. This hang tag is printed one color on self-adhesive plastic stock so that it doubles as a sticker—a popular decorative item with youngsters—after purchase.

▲ **Phone Card** package for **Seiko Instruments**. Design Firm: **Stan Evenson Design;** Art Director/ Designer: **Stan Evenson**

Phone Card is a card-sized pocket calculator that also functions as a personal telephone directory. Large, brightly-colored numbers call attention to the product's function.

❖ Shoe box for **L.A. Gear.** Design Firm: **Stan Evenson Design;** Art Director: **Stan Evenson;** Designer: **David Sapp**

The "cross connection" is an all-purpose athletic shoe that is a throwback to the time when sneakers came in only two flavors: PF Flyers and Keds. The packaging had to tell buyers how and why this one shoe would fit all of their needs: running, court games and general sporting about town.

■ Product graphics and box for **The Stride Rite Corp.** Design Firm: **Landor Associates, New York;** Art Director/Illustrator: **Karen Correll;** Designers: **Karen Correll, Douglas Lloyd**

The goal was to add fashion and a dash of fun to the respected Stride Rite line of children's footwear.

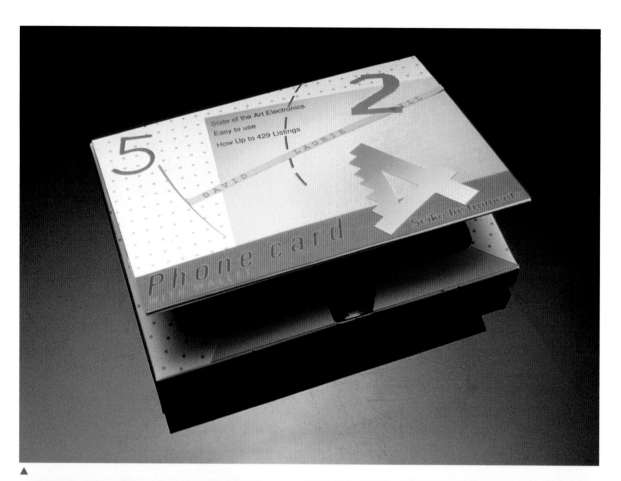

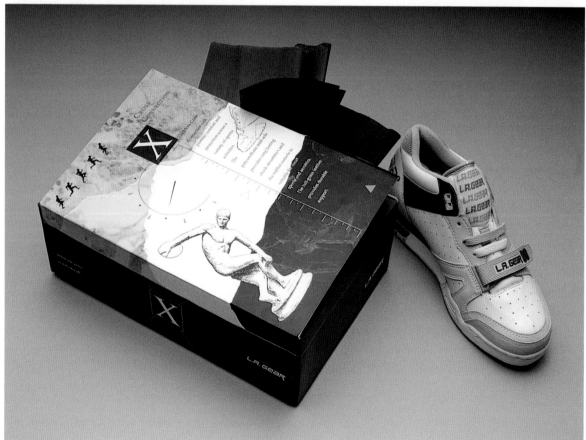

▲ **FinTek Species Kits** for **Berkley.** Design Firm: **SBG Partners;** Art Director: **Courtney Reeser;** Designer: **Tom McNulty;** Illustrator: **Justin Carroll**

The FinTek fishing system consists of a rod, reel and line specially designed for different species of fish. If buyers don't recognize the species by the colorful illustration, the name is displayed in bold type below the product logo.

❖ Sporting goods products packaging for **Wilson Sporting Goods Company.** Design Firm: **Selame Design;** Art Director: **Joe Selame;** Designers: **Selame Design group**

The Wilson logo is recognized around the world. To capitalize on its equity and keep packaging costs low without sacrificing visual impact at retail, Selame Design created a system of modular die-cut packages. These allow the maximum number of facings in a well-stocked sporting goods section. Printed three or four colors on various papers and corrugated stock with foil stamping.

▲

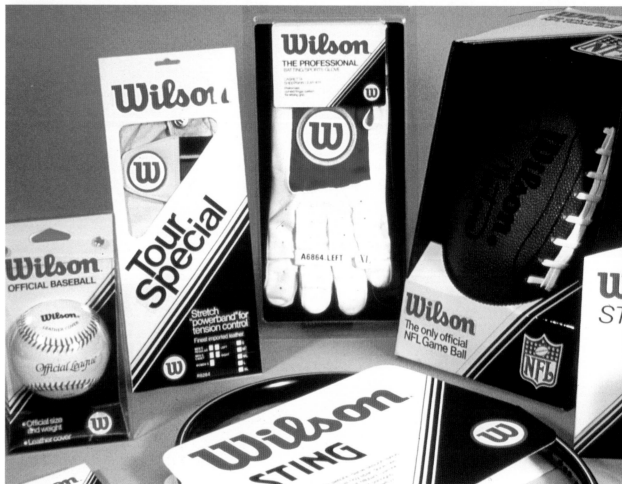

❖

 **Penn Tennis Balls** for **Penn Athletic Products Division.** Design Firm: **Selame Design;** Art Director: **Joe Selame;** Designers: **Selame Design group**

To give Penn tennis balls a more contemporary image, Selame Design updated the Penn signature and set supporting copy in Univers. Variations on a red, yellow and black color scheme differentiate the three products—Penn Medalist, Penn and Pro-Penn. Labels are printed on shrink film by flexography.

● **American Lights** for **The American Tobacco Company.** Design Firm: **Peterson & Blyth;** Art Director: **David Scarlett;** Designer: **Bob Cruanas**

This design launched a new premium quality cigarette from The American Tobacco Company to an enthusiastic market in Japan and Taiwan. A red, white and blue color scheme and an illustration of an eagle capitalizes on the Japanese interest in Americana.

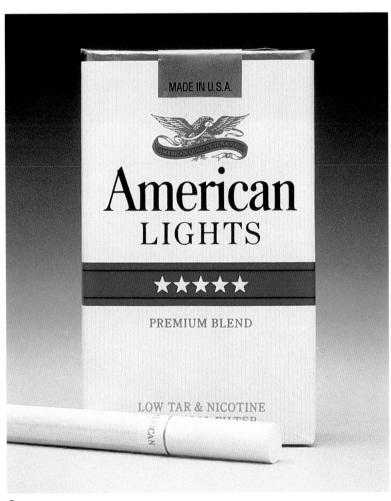

▲ **Malibu Cigarettes** for **The American Tobacco Company.** Design Firm: **Peterson & Blyth;** Art Director: **David Scarlett;** Designer: **Bob Cruanas**

A name of almost mythic significance to young people and bright, tropical colors were used for the launch of this youth-oriented new brand. According to American Tobacco, the look helped make this its most successful new product since the introduction of Carlton more than two decades ago.

❖ **Family Match Darts** for **Lewis Galoob Toys.** Design Firm: **Jamie Davison Design, Inc.;** Art Director: **Jamie Davison;** Designers: **Jamie Davison, Norma Rae Manty**

A bold contemporary look for an old, traditional game was intended to make Family Darts appeal to a wide range of ages.

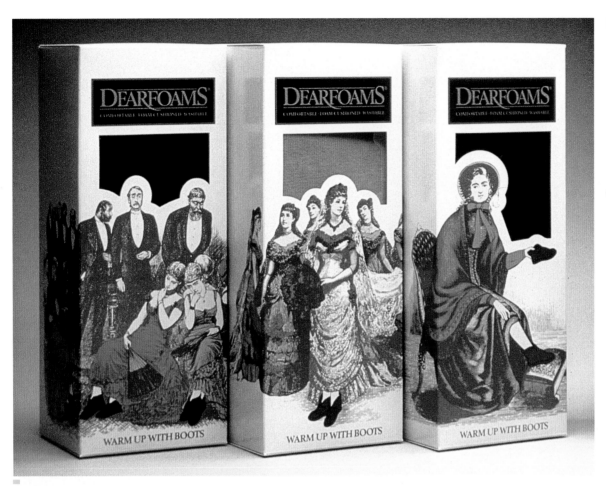

■ **Dear Foams** for **R.G. Barry.** Design Firm: **Peterson & Blyth;** Art Director: **Ronald Peterson;** Designer: **Jacquie Fauter-MacConnell**

A series of charming illustrations rendered to look like antique steel-cut engravings create mini-tableaux when Dear Foams slipper packages are grouped on a shelf.

● Computer products packaging for **Tarsus.** Design Firm: **Pentagraph;** Art Director: **Mark Posnett;** Designer: **Colleen Pote**

A playful use of type lends a unique look to this range of computer products.

▲ **Player's Cigarettes** for **Imperial Tobacco Co.** Design Firm: **Axion Design Inc.;** Art Directors: **Robert P. deVito, Kathleen Keating;** Designer: **Eric Read**

A cult favorite for years, Player's cigarettes were given a face-lift to strengthen their appeal to a wider variety of smokers. The white background also implies a lighter smoke—an important message to today's health-conscious consumers.

❖ **Boule D'Or Plus** cigarettes for **B.A.T.-Benelux.** Design Firm: **Design Board Behaeghel & Partners;** Designer/Illustrator: **Johan Corvers;** Art Director: **Denis Keller**

This new symbol and package were created for the introduction of a crush-proof box for Boule D'Or Plus cigarettes.

▨ **Harley-Davidson** cigarettes for **Lorillard**. Design Firm: **Mittleman/Robinson Design Associates;** Art Director/Designer: **Fred Mittleman**

Targeted to men ages 21 to 35, Lorillard asked for an adaptation of the Harley-Davidson motorcycle logo that would portray an image of strength and quality.

▲ Label graphics for AM/FM card-size radio manufactured by **Casio Computer Co., Ltd.** Design Firm: **Kaneko Design Office;** Art Director: **Tomihiro Kaneko;** Designers: **Kaneko Design Office staff**

With space at a premium, the studio used color bands and geometric shapes in different configurations for this line of credit card size electronics goods.

❖ **Ty-D-Bol Toilet Cleaner** for **Kiwi Brands.** Design Firm: **JS Mandle & Company, Inc.;** Art Director: **James Mandle;** Designer: **Matt Mattus**

Too many words and a lack of focus rendered the old Ty-D-Bol label ineffective, despite the presence of the endearing Ty-D-Bol man. A revitalized graphic treatment featuring a contemporary rendering of the Ty-D-Bol man brand mark and less copy both clarified and strengthened the sales message.

■ **Super Kem-Tone** paints for **Dutch Boy Group.** Design Firm: **Promanad Communication, Inc.;** Art Director/Designer: **Peter Land;** Printer: **Sherwin-Williams/Graphic Arts Printing**

Increasing competition from private-label paints encouraged Sherwin-Williams Company to strengthen the presentation of its Super Kem-Tone line. A stronger logo was developed and used to anchor this five-color label.

● **Manor Hall** paints for **Pittsburgh Paints.** Design Firm: **Libby Perszyk Kathman;** Art Director: **John Metz;** Designer: **Susan Bailey Zinader;** Illustrator: **Bill Ellison.**

An upscale label design featuring the Pittsburgh Paints logo launched this line of premium house paints.

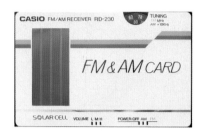

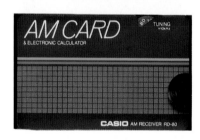

▲

❖

■

●

Great Life exterior paint for **Martin-Senour Company.** Design Firm: **Promanad Communication, Inc.;** Art Director/Designer: **Peter Land;** Printer: **Sherwin-Williams/Graphic Arts Printing**

This premium exterior paint line needed a strong presentation to convince buyers of its superiority. Six color printing was combined with matte and gloss varnishes to enhance the graphics.

True Grip floor treatment for **Pacific Specialty Chemical, Inc.** Design Firm: **Image Group, Inc.;** Art Director/Designer: **Mark Marinozzi;** Illustrators: **Mark Marinozzi, Brad Mager;** Production: **Brad Mager**

True Grip is a line of industrial products that create a slip-retardant surface on floors. Contemporary packaging graphics that incorporate graduated color bands and an intriguing logo create a brand identity and call attention to the problem of slippery floors. The grid behind the words "True Grip" symbolizes a non-skid surface.

▲ **Clear Wood Preservative** for the **Dutch Boy Group.** Design Firm: **North Star;** Designer: **Dick Sidman;** Printer: **Sherwin-Williams/Graphic Arts Printing**

Lush six-color printing was used to help launch this new line of wood preservatives that would compete with established national brands. The large illustrations show immediately the many areas of a house that can benefit from preservative treatment.

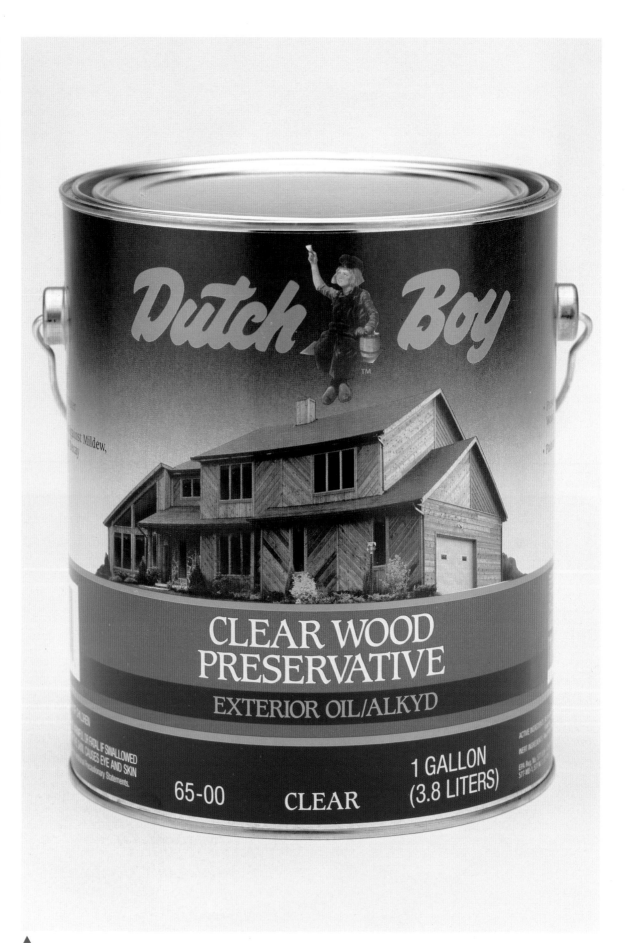

❖ **Free Spirit Interior Enamel** for **Martin-Senour Company**. Design Firm: **Promanad Communications, Inc.;** Art Director/Designer: **Peter Land;** Printer: **Sherwin-Williams/Graphic Arts Printing**

Six colors were also used for the premium paints produced by Martin-Senour, a division of Sherwin-Williams Company. The design was intended to strengthen the buyer's perception of quality and give strong shelf impact.

▪ Building adhesives for **Wascor**. Design Firm: **Platinum Design, Inc.;** Art Director/Designer: **Victoria Peslak**

Basic products in basic black—dressed up with a bow tie. Strong typography makes it unlikely that consumers will pick up the wrong type of adhesive.

● **Ganahl Paint** for **Ganahl Lumber Co.** Design Firm: **Stan Evenson Design**; Art Director/Designer: **Stan Evenson**

Founded in 1884, Ganahl Lumber Co. is an upscale hardware and home improvement store. For its private label paints, the store sought a name and look that would exploit the equity of its long history.

▲ Stockings packaging for **Armani.** Design Firm: **Michael Peters + Partners;** Art Director/Designer: **Maddy Bennett**

Elegance through simplicity. The focal point of this sophisticated design is the triangle-shaped hole created when the flaps are folded to secure the package. In keeping with the minimalist approach, the only other element on the package is the Giorgio Armani logo.

❖ **Dulux** paint for **ICI Australia Limited.** Design Firm: **Cato Design Inc.;** Designers: **Cato Design Inc.**

The different photographs on these paint can labels act as a "home decorator's guide," giving consumers ideas on how to use the paint in their homes.

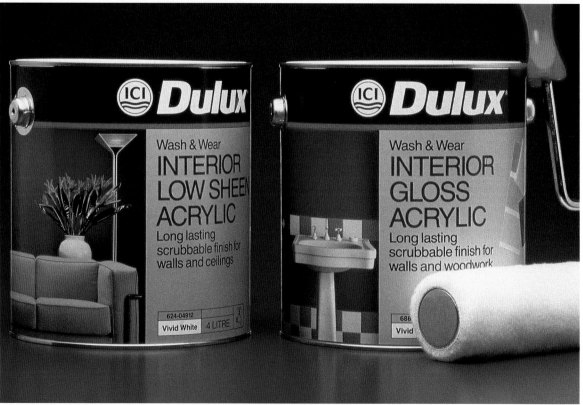

Cento for **Johnson Wax.** Design Firm: **VU srl;** Art Director/Illustrator: **Gianni Parlacino;** Designer: **Annalisa Papa**

A high-tech look for this Johnson Wax cleaning product sold in Italy. Bright bands of color set at an angle contrast with the strong vertical lines of the center white panel. The white cap, cut at angles to expose the spray nozzle, continues the geometric lines of the design.

▲ **Zin** liquid laundry products for **Pau de Açùar Group.** Design Firm: **Dil Publicidade Ltda.**

Extensions to a line of private-label home products manufactured in Brazil, the labels for Zin had to follow the curves of the container. The bottle shape was determined from both ergonomic studies and by the needs of the factory filling line. Pigments were added to the bottle material to differentiate each variety.

◆ **Ultramax** soaps for **Ultramax S.A.** Design Firm: **Estudio Hache;** Designers: **Laura Lazzeretti, Marcelo Varela;** Illustrator: **Miriam Obregon**

Clear bottles allow the color of each product—dyed to match its scent—to differentiate these varieties of cleaning solution.

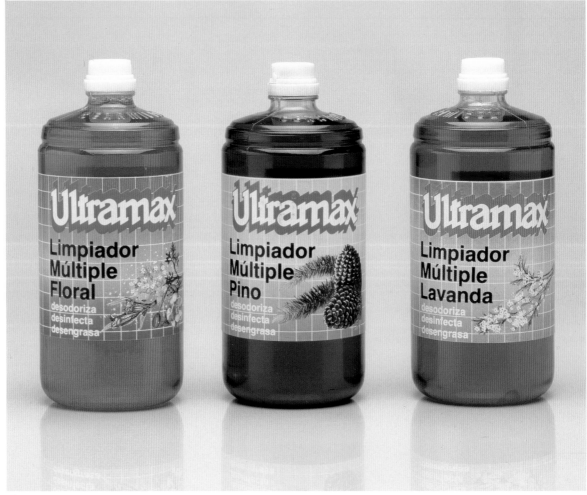

■ **Arm & Hammer Liquid Laundry Soap** for **Church & Dwight.** Design Firm: **JS Mandle & Company, Inc.;** Art Director: **Janet Umland;** Designers: **Sean Carter, Mark Pierce**

Church & Dwight sought to modernize the image of its Arm & Hammer laundry detergent without making it appear to be a premium, higher-price product. Significant equity in the well-known logo was preserved by making it the focal point of the redesign.

▲ **Lawn Restore** for **Ringer**. Design Firm: **Designed Marketing** Art Director/Designer: **Tim Moran**; Illustrator: **Kim Behm**

Containing organic ingredients, rather than chemicals, Lawn Restore required room for sales copy on the front of the packaging to explain the product's benefits and justify its higher price.

◆ Identity for **RareWoods**. Design Firm: **Jamie Davison Design, Inc.;** Art Director: **Jamie Davison;** Designers: **Jamie Davison, Tia Stoller**

The designers' goal was a handmade look that would convey the craftsmanship of Rare-Woods' line of fine wooden picture frames.

■ Seed bags for **Sacramento Valley Milling**. Design Firm: **Image Group, Inc.;** Art Director/Designer/Illustrator: **Mike Thomas;** Printing/Film Work: **Bemis Bag Company**

Color codes at the top and bottom of these seed bags make it easy to distinguish the varieties when they are stacked on a pallet. The bags were printed in four PMS colors on kraft paper.

● **Border Patrol** for **Clyde Robin's Seed Company**. Design Firm: **SBG Partners;** Art Director/Designer: **Barbara Vick;** Illustrator: **Dave Stevenson**

Fighting flower pests with flowers is a somewhat novel idea. The label for Border Patrol had to project that it is a serious botanical product while also showing the beauty of the flowers it produces.

▲

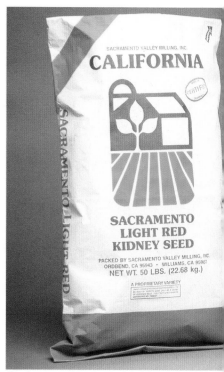

◆

■

▲ **Bosch** electric tools for **Robert Bosch GmbH.** Design Firm: **Knut Hartmann Design;** Art Directors: **Regine Hany, Knut Hartmann;** Designer/Illustrator: **Regine Hany**

This four-color package design has been extended to all Bosch tool packaging.

❖ **Wagner Power Painters** for **Wagner Spray Tech.** Design Firm: **Designed Marketing;** Art Director/Designer: **Bob Upton;** Photographers: **Andy Kingsbury, Glen Silker**

A strong yellow and black logo is the unifying graphic element for this extensive line of painting tools. Products are shown spraying, rolling or scraping the yellow band of the logo. Printed five colors with a varnish. The design was also applied to boxes, packaging sleeves, blister packs and hanging cartons.

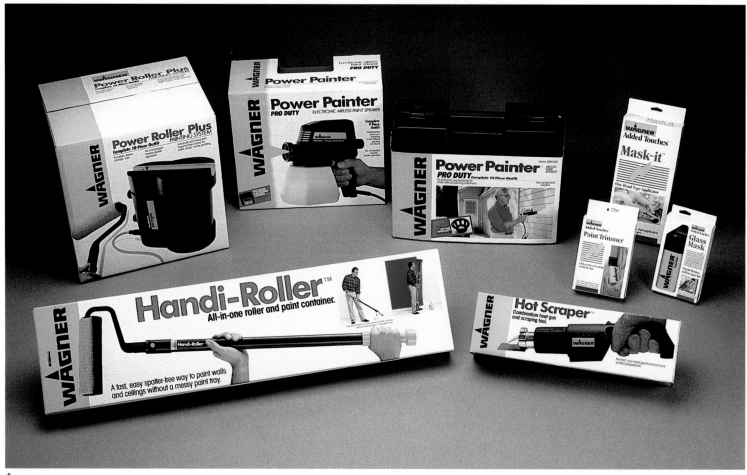

LiteSet Miniature Telephone Headset for **Plantronics.** Design Firm: **Axion Design Inc.;** Art Director: **Robert P. deVito;** Designer: **Eric Read**

This is a refreshing change from the more usual smiling consumer/high-tech look commonly used in the packaging of electronics. The result is a package that has a higher perceived value (and costs less to produce) than a four-color process box.

▲ Packaging for **Avery Consumer Products.** Design Firm: **Bright & Associates;** Art Director: **Keith Bright;** Designer: **Wes Haynes**

Avery commissioned Bright & Associates to design the outer packaging and point-of-purchase displays for its expanded line of easy reference products aimed at students in grades 7-12. Contemporary graphics and bright colors appeal to young buyers, position the products as "user friendly" and differentiate the line from the competition.

❖ Label and packaging graphics for **Champion Spark Plug.** Design Firm: **Design Board Behaeghel & Partners;** Art Director: **Denis Keller;** Designers/Illustrators: **Erik Vantal, Christina Jans**

A color-coded graphic system featuring product graphics was applied to Champion's new line of car care products.

■ Stereo Head Phones packaging for **Nippon Columbia Co., Ltd.** Design Firm: **Kaneko Design Office;** Art Director: **Tomihiro Kaneko;** Designers: **Kaneko Design Office staff**

Design specifications called for outer packaging that would show the merchandise and position the product as a high-end item. The gold type is hot-stamped onto the transparent vinyl casing.

● Voltage Valet™ Travel Appliances for **Hybrinetics, Inc.** Design Firm: **Image Group, Inc.;** Art Directors: **Tom Armstrong, Mark Marinozzi;** Designer: **Chris Cornelssen.**

Diagonal color bands highlight and underline the product name. Four-color photographs are set against a black graduated dot screen to give them some dimension. The back panel consists of promotional copy and instructions on how to use the appliance. Printed in four colors on 20-point SBS stock with a UV coating.

☆ **Natural Animal Flea Powder** for **Ecosafe.** Design Firm: **American Design;** Art Director: **Jill Finche-Graham;** Designer: **Gary Crane**

Earthy colors were selected for these natural pet care items, sold primarily in natural foods stores. Printed in four colors on glossy label stock.

▲ **Brake Shoes** for **Bendix.** Design Firm: **Selame Design;** Art Director: **Joe Selame;** Designers/Illustrators: **Selame Design Group**

Previously, Bendix brake products were stocked behind the automotive parts counter. The new and relined products featured here are merchandised on store shelves and required distinctive graphics. The package design appeals to do-it-yourself consumers with informative copy that emphasizes product benefits. Color-coded bands identify the brake materials (metallic, organic, and so on). Printed four color on corrugated paper.

❖ **Probe** herbicide for **Sandoz Crop Protection.** Design Firm: **Peterson & Blyth;** Art Director: **Ronald Peterson;** Designers: **Peterson & Blyth**

A bold presentation launched this new line of herbicides. Illustrations of the kinds of weeds Probe controls clearly communicate the product's function. The design program—featuring a pictorial, strong brand name and bold blue band—can easily be adapted to new products as they're introduced.

■ **Valvoline Motor Oil** for **Valvoline Division, Ashland Oil.** Design Firm: **Libby Perszyk Kathman;** Art Director/Illustrator: **Howard McIlvain**

The one-quart bottles are the primary vehicle in a bold, dynamic brand identity system that presents the company as a leading-edge technology petroleum products manufacturer.

▲

❖

■

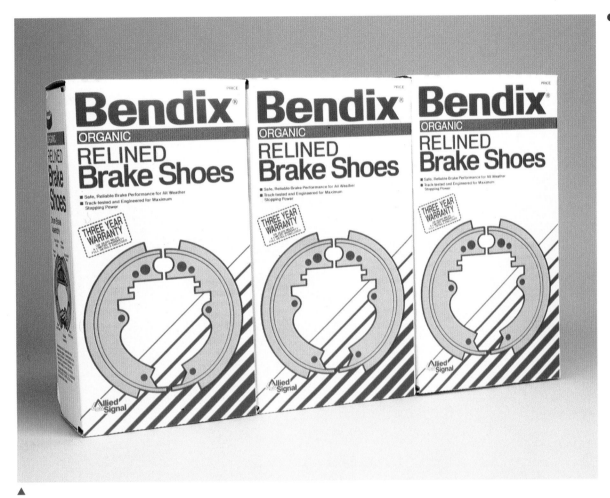

▲

●

Motor oils for **Amoco Oil Corporation.** Design Firm: **Selame Design;** Art Director: **Joe Selame;** Designers: **Selame Design Group**

The newest design in Amoco's extensive line of private label motor oil promotes the brand's retail identity as well as the corporate colors. Design elements were angled to imply motion. Printed four color offset on label stock for metal cans and one-quart plastic containers.

MEDIA PRODUCTS

It is positively entertaining to watch as the frontiers of design range across the marketing landscape. The mid-1980s produced a bumper crop of record album jackets that were stunning and trend-setting. It seems that just as the genre reached its peak, the market threw its practitioners a curve ball: the compact disc. Images intended to be shown full bleed on the jacket for a twelve-inch LP had to be shrunk down to the size of a four-by-five inch transparency.

The high-tech wave crested in the mid-1980s as well, evidenced in such memorable packaging as the line of magnetic tapes from 3M Corp.

The packaging of computer software seems to be the heir to these diverse design legacies. Not only has the number of micro-computers in use increased dramatically, but the number of new software programs has exploded. At the same time, software—once sold on the personal recommendation of small dealerships—is now sold in dedicated software retail outlets, in office supply stores and, increasingly, by direct mail. These channels of distribution demand that the graphics be sharp and that the packaging communicate the power and utility of the programs. In terms of design, the category hasn't found its feet quite yet. As one observer put it: "If I see one more grid going off into space with a sphere floating on it...." ♦

Software will likely be this decade's wunderkind. Although bright colors and shapes have been tried, muted tones and a more restrained approach seem destined to prevail.

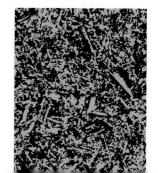

▲ **Steve Miller "Born 2B Blue"** for **Capitol Records.** Design Firm: **Stan Evenson Design;** Art Director/Designer: **Stan Evenson**

When rocker Steve Miller changed his sound for a mellower, jazz-influenced album he decided it should be called "Born 2B Blue." Stan Evanson Design translated this title into a contemporary package that still reflects the best imagery of the Jazz Age. The look was then adapted for use on compact discs and cassette tapes.

❖ **Catalog** for **Dagbladunie.** Design Firm: **Samenwerkende Ontwerpers;** Art Director: **Andre Toet;** Designer: **Jan-Paul de Vries**

The usual catalog treatment—simple self-cover—is abandoned for a layered, multi-element package. An outer cardboard shipping carton is die-cut to display the graphic on the front of a slipcase, which contains a catalog wrapped in white paper.

▲

❖

Finale Music Software for **Wenger Corp.** Design Firm: **The Duffy Design Group;** Art Director/Designer: **Joe Duffy;** Illustrators: **Joe Duffy, Lynn Shulte**

Finale is a unique music software package that allows musicians to score music on a Macintosh computer. A miniature piano keyboard plugs into the computer and the composer "plays" the piece on the keyboard. The software package records this performance and generates sheet music duplicating the performance. Because this product is so unusual, it needed an elaborate package to highlight its features at the point of sale and house the many components. A slipcase holds the instruction manual, software diskettes and instructional videotape. When the manual is pulled from the slipcase, the composer at the piano—printed on the outside of the case—changes to the composer at a keyboard, printed on the manual. The opposite transition takes place on the other side of the package. The package is printed in six colors and wrapped over board stock.

▲ Videotapes for **Fallon McElligott**. Design Firm: **The Duffy Design Group;** Art Director/Designer: **Sharon Werner;** Illustrators: **S. Werner, L. Schulte**

Fallon McElligott, a Minneapolis-based advertising agency, asked The Duffy Design Group to create a package for a videotape that would be given to agency employees and clients at Christmas. The tape contains copies of the agency's best television commercials from the preceding year. A few months later, Fallon McElligott recut the tape, adding a discussion of how advertising works for companies. This new tape was given a similar package and distributed to members of the Young President's Organization.

❖ **R:Base** software for **Microrim**. Design Firm: **Hornall Anderson Design Works;** Art Director: **Jack Anderson;** Designers: **Jack Anderson, Luann Bice, Paula Cox**

For its popular R:Base database software, Microrim asked for an approach that was a departure from the company's existing package. A four-color slip wrapper was designed to fit over a two-color linen box.

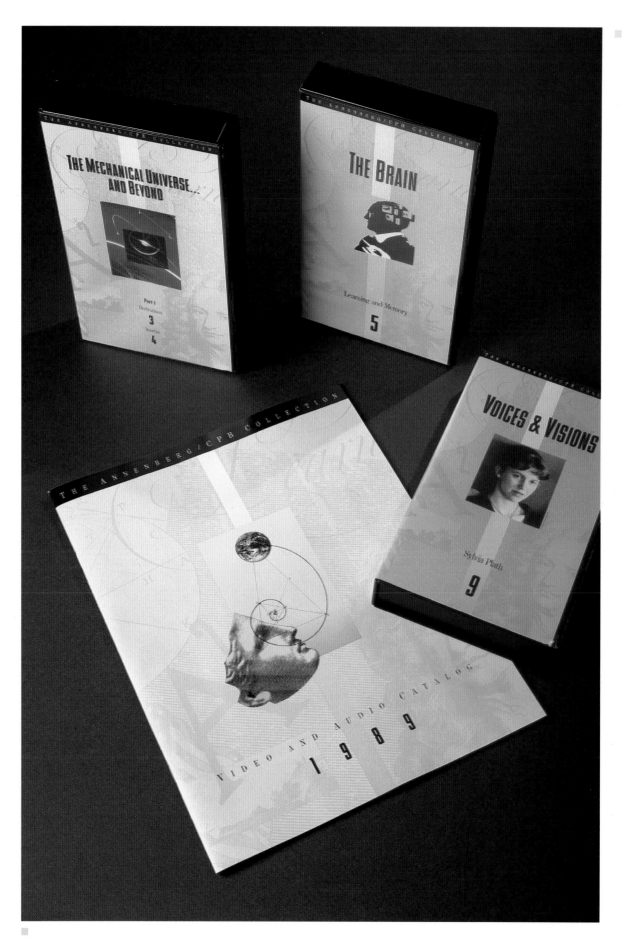

Videotapes and catalog for **The Annenberg Foundation.** Design Firm: **Gerald Reis & Company;** Art Director: **Gerald Reis;** Designers: **Gerald Reis, Albert Treskin**

The Annenberg Foundation offers a series of educational videotapes on science, math, the humanities and the social sciences. In its packaging for the materials, Gerald Reis & Company created a tapestry of etched images of elements drawn from each of these categories. This tapestry was used as a background for the packages. Each category was then given its own color palette and a unique visual to serve as an identifier.

▲ Media products for **Kodak.** Design Firm: **Selame Design;** Art Director: **Joe Selame;** Designers: **Selame Design Group**

Kodak sells a bewildering variety of products in virtually every country in the world. Individual identities were created for these media products, yet all carry a visual relationship to the strong Kodak corporate mark and to each other. The use of yellow, black and red is an "automatic" as those are Kodak's house colors; in the photographic retail trade, its products are known as "yellow box items."

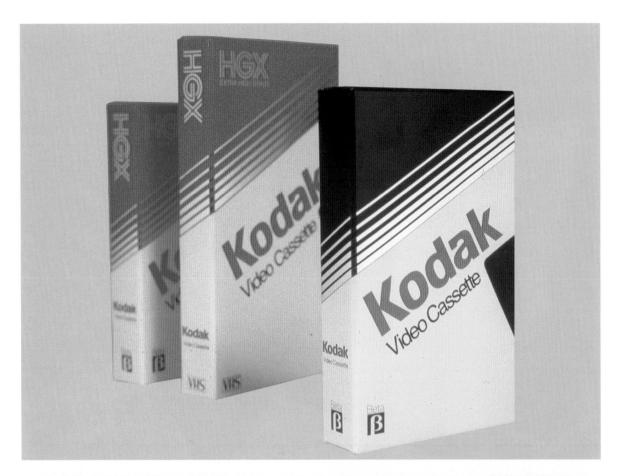

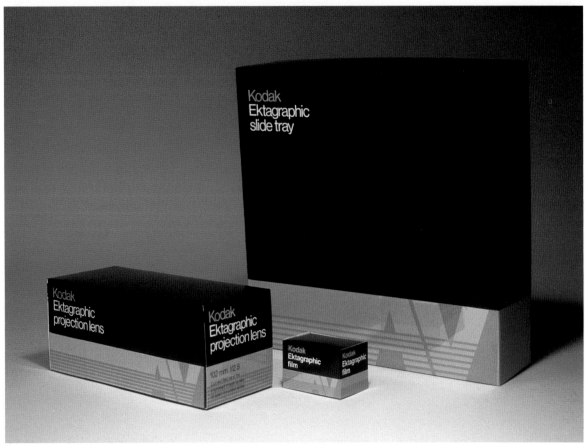

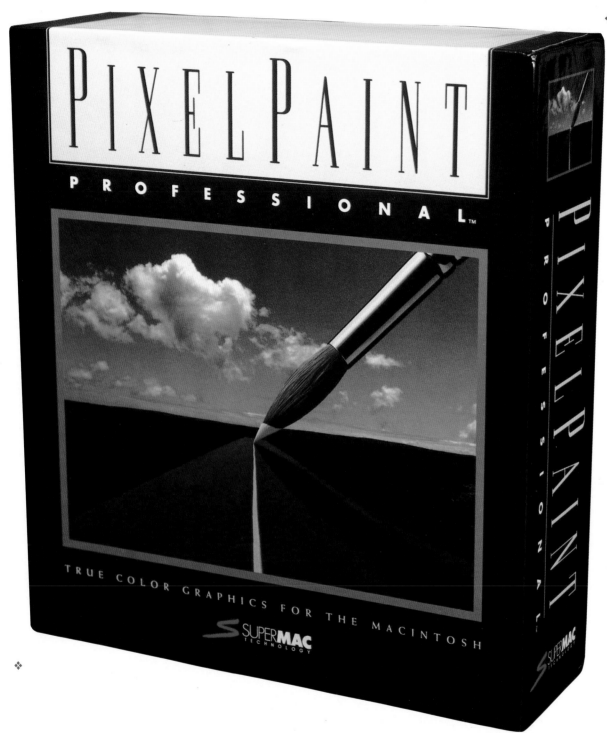

SuperMac sells two different versions of its Pixel Paint image-manipulation software for the Macintosh computer. For the Pixel Paint Professional version, Primo Angeli Inc. created a stunning concept illustration that immediately identifies the purpose of the software and suggests its esthetic and technical power. The legend "True Color Graphics..." below the illustration points out that the package works with photographic-quality 24-bit digital color images. The illustration was created on a Macintosh computer using Pixel Paint Professional software.

▲ **Memorex HBS Series Audio Tapes** for **Memtek Products.** Design Firm: **Axion Design Inc.;** Art Director: **Robert P. de Vito;** Designer: **Eric Read**

There once was one brand of audio cassettes and it was made in Minnesota. Today, there are not only a plethora of brands—ranging from European to East Asian and everything in between—there are also many different kinds of audio tape. Axion created a strong graphic system for Memorex that clearly ties its products into a family line, yet allows enough diversity to communicate the differences between the tape varieties.

❖ **Instant Synthesizer** for **Electronic Arts.** Design Firm: **Jamie Davison Design, Inc.;** Art Director: **Jamie Davison;** Designers: **Jamie Davison, Norma Rae Manty;** Photographer: **Thomas Heinser**

A reversal of the usual motto "Out of Many, One," Instant Synthesizer is a software product that allows a computer to mimic many different musical instruments from a single keyboard. The creative freedom this allows musicians is expressed in the free-form graphics, while a variety of musical instruments clearly communicates the software's purpose.

▩ **Gold Works** for **Gold Hill Computers.** Design Firm: **Selame Design;** Art Director: **Joe Selame;** Designers: **Selame Design Group**

Gold Works is a top-of-the-line artificial intelligence software development product which needed a package design that was as sophisticated and high-tech looking as the product. Selame Design abandoned the severe geometric shapes found on many software packages, opting instead for a "soft" illustration rendered in muted shades of gray. Four special match colors were printed on a special plasticized stock laminated on chip board to create the seven shades of gray. The brand mark was stamped in gold foil.

Akagi Design
17 Osgood Place
San Francisco, CA 94133
(415) 397-4668

Shigeru Akizuki
815, 4-27-32 Ikejiri
Setagaya-ku, Tokyo 154 Japan
(03) 412-1371

Alan Chan Design Co.
Rm. 801-2 Shui Lam Bldg.
23 Luard Rd.
Wanchai, Hong Kong
(852) 5-278228

Alternatives
236 W. 27th St.
New York, NY 10001
(212) 243-1099

American Bank Note Holographics
500 Executive Blvd.
Elmsford, NY 10523
(914) 582-2355

American Design
414 S. 8th St.
Livingston, MT 59047
(406) 222-7272

Andrew Bell Graphic Designers Pty Ltd.
6/310 Beaconsfield Parade
Middle Park, Victoria, Australia 3206
(03) 537-1219

Apple Design Source
305 E. 46th St., Floor 4
New York, NY 10017
(212) 758-9292

Axion Design Inc.
Box 629
San Anselmo, CA 94960
(415) 258-6800

The Berni Corporation
666 Steamboat Rd.
Greenwich, CT 06830
(203) 661-4747

Bright & Associates
3008 Main St.
Santa Monica, CA 90405
(213) 450-2488

Broom & Broom
99 Green St.
San Francisco, CA 94111
(415) 397-4300

Butler/Kosh/Brooks
940 N. Highland Ave., #C
Los Angeles, CA 90038
(213) 469-8128

Cato Design Inc. Pty. Ltd.
254 Swan St.
Richmond, Victoria, 3121 Australia
(03) 429-6577

Clifford Selbert Design
2067 Massachusetts Ave.
Boston, MA 02140
(617) 497-6605

Colonna, Farrell: Strategic Marketing & Design
1335 Main St.
St. Helena, CA 94574
(707) 953-2077

Congdon Macdonald Inc.
420 Lexington Ave., Suite 2046
New York, NY 10170
(212) 697-9300

Margaret Cusack
Margaret & Frank & Friends Inc.
124 Hoyt St.
Brooklyn, NY 11217
(718) 237-0145

DeFELICE Enterprises Inc.
136-G Research Dr.
Milford, CT 06460
(203) 877-9697

Design Board/Behaeghel & Partners
Avenue Georges Lecointe 50
1180 Brussels, Belgium
32-2-375 39 62

The Design Company
93 Summer St., Suite 200
Boston, MA 02110
(617) 338-0974

Designed Marketing
2500 Foshay Tower
Minneapolis, MN 55402
(612) 340-0333

DIL Publicidade Ltda.
Rue Sete de Abril
261 12 Floor, CEP 01043
Sao Paulo, Brazil

The Duffy Design Group
701 Fourth Ave. South
Minneapolis, MN 55415
(612) 339-3247

Dutch Boy Group
101 Propsect Ave.
15 Midland Bldg.
Cleveland, OH 44115
(216) 566-3300

Eden Foods
701 Tecumseh Rd.
Clinton, MI 49236
(517) 456-7457

Elmwood Design Ltd.
Elmwood House, Ghyll Road,
Guiseley, Leeds
West Yorkshire, LS20 9LT, England
(0943) 870229

Estudio Canovas
Mexico 547 1 "B"
1097 Buenos Aires, Argentina
30-4939

Estudio Hache
Arcos 2680
1428 Buenos Aires, Argentina
781-2408

Frazier Design
1275 Folsom St.
San Francisco, CA 94103
(415) 863-9613

Gerald Reis & Co.
560 Sutter St.. Suite 301
San Francisco, CA 94102
(415) 421-1232

Giancarlo Marchi Design
Via L. Rizzo 81
Perugia, Italy
(0039) 075/5000I7I

Graphic Partners
Gladstone Court
179 Canongate
Edinburgh, Lothian,
EH8 8BN Scotland

The Graphics Studio
811 North Highland Ave.
Los Angeles, CA 90038
(213) 466-2666

Hans Flink Design
7-11 S. Broadway #401
White Plains, NY 10601
(914) 328-0888

Harte Yamashita & Forest
5735 Melrose Ave.
Los Angeles, CA 90038
(213) 462-6486

Hillis, Mackey & Company
1550 Utica Ave. South
Minneapolis, MN 55416
(612) 542-9122

The Hively Agency
520 Post Oak Ave., Suite 800
Houston, TX 77027
(713) 961-2888

Hornall Anderson Design Works
108 Western Ave., Suite 600
Seattle, WA 98104
(206) 467-5800

Image Group
330 Wall St., Suite 5
Chico, CA 95928
(916) 893-4441

Jamie Davison Design
2325 Third St., Suite 339
San Francisco, CA 94107
(415) 864-5775

J.S. Mandle & Company
300 Forest Ave.
P.O. Box 1248
Paramus, NJ 07652
(201) 967-7900

Joel Bronz Design
39 E. 63rd St., Suite 5
New York, NY 10021
(212) 980-1133

John Haag Design
2097 Market St., Suite 30
San Francisco, CA 94114
(415) 864-2471

Kan Tai-keung Design & Associates Ltd.
22 Floor On Loong Comm. Bldg.
276-278 Lockhart Rd.
Wanchai, Hong Kong
(5) 748399

Kaneko Design Office
Long Isle Ikebukuro 501
2-16-22 Mejiro
Toshima-ku, Tokyo, 171 Japan
03-985-9035

Knut Hartmann Design
Corneliusstrasse 8
Frankfurt, W. Germany 6000
(069) 74-7963

Kornick Lindsay Inc.
161 East Erie St.
Chicago, IL 60611
(312) 280-8664

Landor Associates/New York
46 East 61st St.
New York, NY 10021
(212) 751-6961

Lanny Sommese Design
481 Glenn Rd.
State College, PA 16803
(814) 238-7484

Libby Perszyk Kathman
225 E. Sixth St.
Cincinnati, OH 45202
(513) 241-6330

Maeda Design Associates
Sanei Bldg. 8F,
3-20-9 Toyosaki
Kita-ku, Osaka, 531 Japan
(06) 374-0133

Michael Peters & Partners, Ltd.
3 Olaf St.
London, W11 4BE, England
229 3424

Milton Glaser Inc.
E. 32nd St.
New York, NY 10016
(212) 889-3161

Mittleman/Robinson Design Associates
3 West 18th St., Second Floor
New York, NY 10011
(212) 627-5050

Ortega Design
1735 Spring St., P.O. Box 84
St. Helena, CA 94574
(707) 963-3539

Pentagraph Pty. Ltd.
Wolseley Road
Woodmead, Sandton
P.O. Box 745
Sunninghill, 2157 South Africa
(011) 803-5815

Peterson & Blyth Associates Inc.
216 E. 45th St.
New York, NY 10017
(212) 557-5566

Phillips Design Group
25 Drydock Ave.
Boston, MA 02210
(617) 423-7676

Platinum Design Inc.
123 54th St. #3C
New York, NY 10022
(212) 750-5070

Prepared Products Co.
6200 East Flauson Ave.
Los Angeles, CA 90040
(800) 722-3462

Primo Angeli Inc.
590 Folsom St.
San Francisco, CA 94105
(415) 974-6100

Raymond Bennett Design Assoc. Pty. Ltd.
5/9 Myrtle Street
Crows Nest NSW, Australia 2065
(02) 959-5777

Rene Yung Communications Design
466 Green St., Suite 201
San Francisco, CA 94133
(415) 956-6293

Robert P. Gersin Associates
11 E. 22nd North
New York, NY 10010
(212) 777-9500

Robert Pecota Winery
P.O. Box 303
Calistoga, CA 94515
(707) 942-6625

Ruenitz & Company
50 Washington St.
Norwalk, CT 06854
(203) 855-8281

Samenwerkende Ontwerpers
Herengracht 160
1016 BN Amsterdam, The Netherlands
020-240547

San Angel Authentica Salsa
RR2, Box 1390
Stowe, VT 05672
(802) 253-8117

SBG Partners
1725 Montgomery
San Francisco, CA 94111
(415) 931-7500

Selame Design Assoc.
2330 Washington St.
Newton Lower Falls, MA 02162
(617) 969-3150

Candice Silva
26 Victorian Dr.
Old Bridge, NJ 08857
(201) 360-9649

Stan Evenson Design Inc.
4445 Overland Ave.
Culver City, CA 90230
(213) 204-1995

Story's Gourmet Foods Inc.
Box 13
Wolf Island, MO 63881
(314) 649-5621

Taylor/Christian Advertising
8035 Broadway
San Antonio, TX 78209
(512) 829-1700

Tharp Did It
Fifth University Ave., Suite 21
Los Gatos, CA 95030
(408) 354-6726

The Thompson Design Group
524 Union St.
San Francisco, CA 94133
(415) 982-5827

Tim Girvin Design Inc.
911 Western Ave., Suite 408
Seattle, WA 98104-1031
(206) 623-7808

Total Design by
Van Diemenstraat 200
1013 CP, Amsterdam, The Netherlands
(0)20 24 74 96

Tracy Sabin, Illustration & Design
13476 Ridley Rd.
San Diego, CA 92129
(619) 484-8712

Uncle Bum's Food Products
1111 Rancho Conejo Blvd., Suite 204
Newbury Park, CA 91320
(805) 499-5449

Vardimon/Adler Studios
87 Shlomo Hamelech St.
Tel Aviv, 64512, Israel
03-239361

Vu SRL
Via Manzoni 39
Milano, Italy 20121
(02) 6597209

Walcott-Ayers & Shore
505 Seventeenth Ave., Suite 301
Oakland, CA 94612
(415) 444-5204

Wallace Church Associates
330 E. 48th St., 1st Floor
New York, NY 10017
(212) 755-2903

The Weller Institute for the Cure of Design Inc.
P.O. Box 726
1398 Aerie Dr.
Park City, UT 84060-1726
(801) 649-9859

WRK, Inc.
602 Westport Rd.
Kansas City, MO 64111
(816) 561-4189

Also Available From Rockport Publishers

Rockport Publishers Inc.
5 Smith St., Rockport, MA 01966
(508) 546-9590 • FAX: (508) 546-7141

DESIGNS FOR MARKETING NO. 1: PRIMO ANGELI

Edited by Steve Blount & Lisa Walker
Journey with this premiere graphic designer as he traces the development of his well-known commercial designs—including DHL, TreeSweet, Cambridge, Henry Weinhard beer, California Cooler—from initial client meetings to the finished designs. Packed with more than 300 four-color photographs and accompanied by lively text, this is an essential reference for graphic artists and marketers.
144 pages   ISBN 0-935603-10-7
$27.95   Hardcover

THE BEST OF AD CAMPAIGNS!

by Steve Blount & Lisa Walker
Get a behind-the-scenes look at the creation of more than 30 of the best recent international, national and local advertising campaigns, including California Raisin Advisory Board, Chevrolet, Diet Coke, Isuzu, Michelob, Pepsi-Cola and Visa USA. One-on-one interviews with the marketing directors of leading corporations and their ad agencies reveal how each campaign was conceived, the marketing strategy behind the advertising and why the campaign works. Produced in association with the Creative Committee of the American Association of Advertising Agencies.
256 pages   ISBN 0-935603-09-3
$49.95   Hardcover

BEST OF SCREEN PRINTING DESIGN

by Lisa Walker & Steve Blount
A showcase for excellence in graphics of all types, Screen Printing Design is the first book devoted exclusively to silk screened work—from retail advertising to fine art; posters to sportswear; corporate promotions to limited edition serigraphs. More than 400 photos represent the best current screen printed work of graphic designers, illustrators, artists and screen printers worldwide, both in visual design and technique.
240 pages   ISBN 0-935603-17-4
$49.95   Hardcover

TYPE & COLOR: A Handbook of Creative Combinations

Technological innovations in printing, computer graphics and desktop publishing systems have made the commercial arts environment considerably more competitive. Graphic artists must perform quickly, creatively and accurately. Type & Color enables graphic artists to spec type in color quickly and efficiently. Ten sheets of color type styles printed on acetate overlays can be combined with hundreds of color bars, making it possible to experiment with thousands of color/type combinations right at the drawing board. 160 pages plus 10 pages of acetate overlays.
160 pages   ISBN 0-935603-19-0
$34.95   Hardcover

COLOR SOURCEBOOK 1 A Complete Guide to Using Color In Patterns

Originally published with great success in Japan, Color SourceBook 1 is a treasure trove of ideas for creating color combinations, shapes and patterns. Color concepts under the headings "Natural," "Oriental" and "High Tech" provide interesting and useful color design combinations to help create an appropriate color framework for the designer to work within.
112 pages   ISBN 0-935603-28-X
$15.95   Softcover

COLOR SOURCEBOOK II A Complete Guide to Contemporary Color Schemes

Companion to Color SourceBook I, this volume furnishes the designer with color concepts under the headings "Pop," "Retro-Modern" and "Post Modern."
112 pages   ISBN 0-935603-29
$15.95   Softcover

COLOR HARMONY

A step-by-step guide to choosing and combining colors, Color Harmony includes 1,662 individual color combinations; dozens of full-color photos to show you how your color schemes will look; a four-color conversion chart; 61 full-size color charts and much more.
158 pages   ISBN 0-935603-06-9
$15.95   Softcover

TRADEMARKS & SYMBOLS OF THE WORLD I: The Alphabet In Design

Contains more than 1,700 fascinating designs for the 26 letters of the alphabet.
192 pages   ISBN 4-7601-0451-8
$24.95   Softcover

TRADEMARKS & SYMBOLS OF THE WORLD II: Design Elements

Hundreds of design elements that are perfect for a variety of graphic applications—from logos to signage.
192 pages   ISBN 4-7601-0450-X
$24.95   Softcover

TRADEMARKS & SYMBOLS OF THE WORLD III: Pictogram & Sign Design

This book is packed with 1,800 pictograms and signs from around the world.
232 pages   ISBN 0-935603-30-1
$24.95   Softcover

THE BEST IN MEDICAL ADVERTISING AND GRAPHICS

Four hundred stunning and remarkably ingenious medical ads and illustrations have been compiled in this exceptional book. This must-have reference captures, in full-color, the astounding creativity of a group of graphic arts specialists whose work has never before been seen in such entirety. Included is information on advertising goals and strategies, design objectives, audience targeting and client's restrictions.
256 pages   ISBN 0-935603-20-4
$49.95   Hardcover

INTERNATIONAL LOGOTYPES VOLUME ONE

The first in a two-volume set, International Logotypes Volume One is a collection of logos of a variety of businesses from around the world. This book is an essential reference tool in any design studio and marketing department.
216 pages   ISBN 0-935603-41-7
$24.95   Softcover

TRADEMARKS & SYMBOLS OF THE WORLD 2

This hardbound volume is packed with 5,800 all new illustrations by 1,300 leading designers from 38 countries. Trademarks & Symbols of the World 2 continues and surpasses the tradition of comprehensive illustration begun in the first edition. Included are eloquent alphabets, telling trademarks, unmistakable service and certification marks and clever pictogram and sign designs from all over the world.
416 pages   ISBN 4-7601-0480-1
$89.95   Hardcover

Embossing

Hot Stamping

Flexographic

McCoy Label Company Presents Pressure-Sensitive Labels and Gift Cards for Your Distinctive Packaging.

We understand that your distinctive image is vital to your success. For over 65 years our labels and gift cards have helped companies distinguish their products and packaging from those of their competitors.

Choose from vibrant colors produced by our hot-stamping processes, the detailed artistry of our embossing techniques, or the possibilities provided by our flexographic printing.

Though we can "customize" to most configuration requirements, you'll find we have an extensive line of stock colors, shapes, sizes and materials. Whether you're interested in an exact repeat of your existing label or gift card, or are in need of suggestions and alterations, we can meet your needs. **Call us toll-free today at 800-327-5997 or fax your artwork or sample to 707-762-1253.**

Folded Gift Cards

McCoy Label

We'll make you look great!

1250 Holm Road
Petaluma, California 94954

Design by LaRocca Graphics